CHELSEA

AN ILLUSTRATED HISTORY

CHELSEA

AN ILLUSTRATED HISTORY

SCOTT CHESHIRE

Breedon Books
Publishing Company
Derby

First published in Great Britain by
The Breedon Books Publishing Company Limited
44 Friar Gate, Derby, DE1 1DA
1994. New edition 1997.
This edition 1998

ISBN 1 85983 143 5

Printed and bound by Butler & Tanner Limited, Frome and London.
Covers printed by Lawrence-Allen, Avon, Somerset.

Contents

Introduction...6

A Scottish Terrier And A Few Dry Gingers Set Chelsea On Their Way............................7

Promotion, Relegation And Promotion On The See-saw.............................12

The Khaki Cup Final...22

Hope And Despair Once Again.................................26

The Long Road Back...31

The Glamour Days, But No Success...............................38

The Riddle Remains Unsolved.................................44

Unwanted Interlude...54

Back To Business...59

Enter Ted Drake – And The Championship At Last............69

Too Briefly – Jimmy Greaves.................................80

'The Doc' Brings His Remedy.................................85

All Change Once More...95

The FA Cup At Last...101

A European Crown – And A Return To The Dark Days.............112

Seven Years And Seven Managers.................................123

John Neal, Too Briefly – And Ken Bates Arrives On Stage............135

'Doctor' Campbell Finds The Remedy.................................141

At Least A Stadium In Which To Perform.................................145

Hoddle's Passing Gospel...153

Another Change At The Helm — But Three Major Cups In Twelve Months 162

Introduction

YET again the appearance of an updated edition of *Chelsea: An Illustrated History* coincides with major success for the club. In 1997 it was the FA Cup, coming to Stamford Bridge for only the second time in Chelsea FC's history. Now, the European Cup-winners' Cup (again for the second time) and the Coca-Cola Cup (yet again for the second time, the first being in its unsponsored days as the League Cup), make seven major trophies in the club's 92-year history and, more significantly, the third in 12 months.

The present playing staff is stronger than ever before, Chelsea are one of the most attractive teams in the country, and Stamford Bridge is taking on the appearance of one of the finest stadiums in Britain.

It is hard to imagine that there has ever been a greater transformation in the fortunes of a football club in such a short space of time, thanks to the foresight and drive of its chairman, Ken Bates, aided by such men as Colin Hutchinson and (sadly all too briefly) Matthew Harding.

As was stated in the last edition, while politicians and others in high places wonder just how best to celebrate the Millennium, the 21st century has already arrived at Fulham Road.

And as before, the author wishes to acknowledge the debt he owes to Albert Sewell's *Chelsea Champions* and John Moynihan's *The Chelsea Story*, from both of which he has drawn information.

Thanks are also due to the staff of the publishers, Breedon Books, and to Sally Taylor, who prepared the text of the original book and its update with speed and efficiency.

When this book was first published in 1994, I expressed the hope that the next chronicler of Chelsea FC's history would have the pleasure of recording new and higher achievements. In 1997 I was able to record that this hope had been fulfilled a good deal sooner than even the greatest optimist could have expected. I also asked what could now lie ahead. The immediate answer, of course, was the arrival of two more major cups at Stamford Bridge. So the question has to be asked again. Could the answer now be the Premiership title itself? Chelsea seem well poised for such an assault as the new century dawns.

Scott Cheshire
June 1998

A Scottish Terrier And A Few Dry Gingers Set Chelsea On Their Way

THE curious tale of how Chelsea Football Club was founded has been related many times and is so extraordinary that it is still difficult to accept, even given the many vicissitudes which have befallen the club for over 90 years. Rather, it has proved to be symptomatic of much which has happened since.

Without the commanding presence of the Stamford Bridge Athletic Ground and its unique position in Central London, a mere few minutes travel away from Piccadilly Circus, it is doubtful whether the boundary between the Chelsea and Fulham boroughs would have ever been considered as a suitable area to promote professional football.

It was in April 1877 that the stadium was opened as a home for the London Athletic Club by the Waddell brothers, James and William, after its earlier headquarters at Lillie Bridge proved unsuitable for various reasons.

The Waddells, shrewd and hardened business operators, acquired the Stamford Bridge site, covering 8½ acres, at the time an area given over to market gardening and fruit growing, for the, then, princely sum of £2,599.

Within six years, however, and following financial scandal, James and William Waddell had not only vanished from West London but had left the country altogether, with the London Athletic Club severely in debt.

Fortunately, a Mr Stunt, a keen athletics enthusiast, then acquired the freehold of the grounds to continue the regular staging of events at the stadium which by now had acquired a grandstand pavilion, in the southwest corner of the arena, with seating for 1,000 spectators and excellent facilities for both running and field events.

Stunt, however, was destined to play a minor role in the Chelsea story for he died in 1902 and, in any case, had shown no interest in enlarging the scope of his property to include other sporting attractions.

More far sighted was a certain Frederick Parker, a flamboyant character, popular man, and a starter on the LAC track. Crucially, he was also a close friend of Gus and Joseph Mears, wealthy London business contractors, who shared Parker's ambitions.

Once they had purchased the freehold of Stamford Bridge, in 1904, the Mears brothers moved quickly. Additional land, amounting to some three acres, was purchased and Gus was already dreaming of owning the finest sporting arena in the land with association football figuring at the top of the agenda.

Soon, he had approached Fulham Football Club,

Stamford Bridge Athletic Ground pictured in the 1890s. The Mears brothers purchased the freehold of the ground in 1904 and Gus Mears' dream of owning the finest sporting arena in the land was under way.

with a view to them moving into Stamford Bridge, only to be rebutted by their then chairman, Mr Henry Norris, and this despite an asking rent of £1,500 per annum, a moderate sum even in those days. It was at this stage that Mr Parker became the central figure in the drama.

Weeks earlier, a most attractive offer had come in from the Great Western Railway Company, who wanted to purchase the site for sidings and a coal and goods yard. Indeed, Gus Mears was on the point of abandoning his project, and accordingly had summoned Frederick Parker to a meeting on the Grounds one Sunday morning, in that autumn of 1904.

However, a new figure in the shape of Mears' Scotch terrier, was about to change the course of history. Savagely attacking Parker, as the two men strolled across the turf, and causing his ankle to bleed profusely, Fred exclaimed, "Your dammed dog has bitten me. Scotch terrier. Always bites before he speaks!" Parker's hopping around in considerable pain, but still laughing heartily, so impressed Mears that in a trice he had changed his mind. "Go to the chemist and get that leg seen to and we will meet here at nine tomorrow morning. Then, we will get busy."

And get busy they did. Within days the two had met Archibald Leitch, the highly respected architect of football grandstands up and down the length of Britain, and a 5,000-seater construction to occupy the eastern side of the ground, was agreed. By February 1905 it was under way and vast new bankings on the other three sides of the ground were being built up from thousands of tons of soil and clay excavated during the building of the Piccadilly Line tube and the Kingsway Tramway tunnel. A capacity for 100,000 spectators was envisaged, with the London Athletic Club signing an agreement keeping them at Stamford Bridge until 1912.

But as yet, in view of Fulham's lack of interest, there was no football team in sight, and so the momentous decision to form a new club was taken, with an idea, which many thought far-fetched, of applying for entry to the Southern League in time for the start of the 1905-06 season later in the year, even though Mears had been assured that such an approach would be most unlikely to be considered.

The first official to be appointed was William Lewis, a Brentford director, as secretary. Lewis was well versed in football matters, having at various times also occupied the positions of chairman, manager and secretary of the West London club as well as being a former referee. More importantly, his contacts within the game were considered to be invaluable if the status of the new club was to be recognised and he immediately set about lobbying support from Southern League clubs, only one of which, Southampton, promised their vote in favour.

As yet no name for the newly-born infant had been decided. Although Stamford Bridge was situated just inside the Borough of Fulham, the obvious title, however, was not a serious option, with Fulham

John Tait Robertson, the first manager of Chelsea FC. The Scottish international half-back had plenty of experience of the English game.

Football Club already well established and housed at Craven Cottage, little over one mile away on the banks of the Thames. Kensington FC, London FC, and Stamford Bridge FC were in turn discarded (the last it was thought could be confused with the Yorkshire town of that name). And so, finally, and not perhaps on the most logical of grounds, the name 'Chelsea' was agreed.

The chairman of the club was to be Mr Claude Kirby, with the Mears brothers also on a six-man board of directors. Things were taking shape.

The next step came on 27 March with the announcement that John Tait Robertson had been appointed player-manager for the first season. 'Jock', a Scottish international half-back, aged 28, had had considerable experience of English football with Everton and Southampton, although the main part of his playing career had been with Glasgow Rangers, where he had won 16 international caps as well as three championship medals and a Scottish FA Cup winners' medal. At a salary of £4 per week, he had certainly assumed considerable responsibility.

With the Southern League offering scant encouragement, attention now turned, somewhat optimistically it would seem, to canvassing the Football League for membership. However unpromising things seemed on the surface, Frederick Parker once again appeared, centre stage, in a vital role. On 20 April, he visited the League headquarters at Lytham to meet the League president, Mr J.J.Bentley.

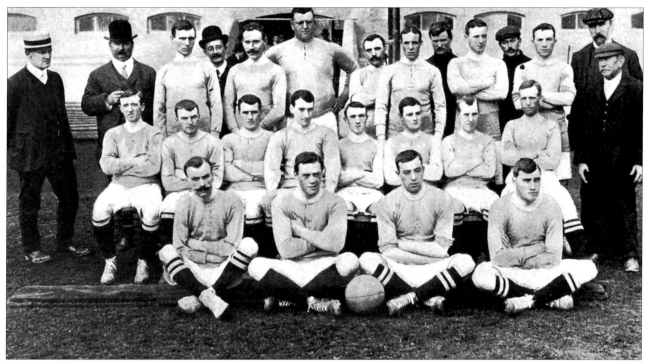

Chelsea's staff in 1905-06. Back row (left to right): J.T.Robertson (manager), H.A. Gus Mears (director), Byrne, Frederick Parker (director), McRoberts, Foulke, Copeland, Mackie, James Miller, McEwan, Harry Ranson (trainer), Craigie, William Lewis (secretary), Jack White (assistant trainer). Middle row: Moran, Donaghy, T.Miller, J.Robertson, O'Hara, Windridge, Key, Kirwan. Front row: Dowland, Slater, Wolff, Watson.

Bentley, far from shutting the door on his approach, remarked to Parker , "Your club is trying to run with the hare and hunt with the hounds. Which are you really going for, the Southern League or us?"

Parker needed no further encouragement. Leaving Bentley's office he telephoned the London Press Agency without further delay and asked them to announce immediately that Chelsea FC was applying for election, not to the Southern League, but to the Football League.

Now it was Robertson's turn to act. Without, as yet, a single player, how could any such application be seriously considered?

Six days later, on 26 April, and with the curtain falling on the 1904-05 season, the first two players were signed. From Small Heath (the club which was later to become Birmingham) came the versatile Bob McRoberts, equally at home at centre-half or centre-forward, and inside-forwards Jimmy Robertson and Jimmy Windridge. Total cost £340! Three weeks on, with the AGM of the Football League fast approaching, another ten names had been added, among them Willie Foulke, Sheffield United's 22st goalkeeper; John Kirwan and David Copeland, Tottenham Hotspur's left-wing pair, and Scotsmen Marshall McEwan (Glasgow Rangers) and Bob Mackie (Heart of Midlothian).

At least Chelsea now had a team and a stadium, but as yet, no league in which to perform.

And yet again, it was Frederick Parker who now took control. On the eve of the Football League AGM, as was only to be expected, much excitement and canvassing from representatives of clubs seeking election, was in evidence. With the time already past 3am and the bar of London's Tavistock Hotel still crowded, Parker, to ensure that his head remained clear for the following day, took the precaution of having a word in the ear of the barmaid so that whenever so many 'Scotch-and-pollies' were ordered, the glass on the left was always a dry ginger. Much of the conversation had been most unfavourable to Chelsea's cause, several clubs showing unwillingness to support a club who had yet to kick ball. "Damned cheek," was the prevalent feeling.

Parker's optimism, however, remained undimmed. Noticing that such remarks were being uttered by managers rather than the chairmen who would be casting the votes, he assured Claude Kirby that there was no cause for worry.

At breakfast Kirby and manager Robertson still exhibited little faith in succeeding and were not to be persuaded by Parker's ebullience. "Bet you each five bob we're elected," he challenged. The wager was accepted and only then did Kirby calmly announce that he had to go his office in the City and was delegating Parker to make the speech to the meeting on Chelsea's behalf.

Totally undeterred and entering the hall whistling and humming, Parker, short and to the point, made three simple points. First, he assured his audience of the financial stability of Chelsea Football Club. Second, he emphasised that Stamford Bridge was a stadium well in keeping with the highest standards in the League. And, finally, he read a list of the players contracted to play for the club.

"Your three minutes are up," announced Mr Bentley. Bowing to the throng, Parker told them, "I thank you for listening so attentively to me and will not trespass on you further beyond suggesting (as he moved towards the door) that when you consider the

Willie Foulke
— Champion Heavyweight

THE name of Foulke may not figure largely in any discussion concerning Chelsea's best-ever goalkeeper, but his name is firmly embedded in the club's history books.

Chelsea's first captain, he remains one of the game's legends. Standing 6ft 6ins in his stocking feet, on his arrival at Stamford Bridge in the summer of 1905 he tipped the scales at 22st. Already past his 30th birthday, and the proud possessor of an England international cap, he was still a fine 'keeper. Often considered a figure of fun, not least by spectators on away grounds, he was held in awe, and respect, by opponents.

High shots and crosses presented little problem. Surprisingly light on his feet, this giant of a man, plucked the ball out of the sky easily enough. 'Shoot low' was the advice given by opposition managers to their forwards. But, even with ground shots he surprised many an attacker with his speed and agility.

Penalty kicks were little problem for him either. Playing for Chelsea against Burton United he saved two spot-kicks, taken by the same player. "You shot straight at him" complained a colleague. "I had to," came the reply. "There was no room on either side."

Until his arrival in London, Willie had spent his entire career with Sheffield United, and after steering Chelsea safely through their first season, he returned to Yorkshire to finish with Bradford City. His time at Bramall Lane had coincided with some of the Blades' greatest days. Apart from his international cap he had two FA Cup winners' medals and a runners-up medal, proof enough of his genuine pedigree.

In addition to being a fine goalkeeper, he was a great character. A man of ready wit and humour who attracted publicity and a host of tales, some of them, no doubt, apocryphal.

He was well known in gentleman's outfitters shops up and down Fulham Road and Kings Road, where he would walk in to enquire for collars. "What size?" he was asked. "Oh, 24s should do, I think", he would retort.

Another often-related story concerned two ticket collectors. On arrival at a northern railway station, somehow Willie became detached from the Chelsea party and, on arrival at the barrier announced that he was 'with the footballers'. The unfortunate officials, totally unconvinced, responded with derisive laughter and refused to let him pass, whereupon Foulke picked them up, tucked one under each arm, and carried them, struggling and protesting, into the station master's office.

One of his Chelsea contemporaries was Martin Moran, the little Scottish winger, at 5ft 4ins the midget of the team. Invariably the two would emerge from the players tunnel side by side to the amusement of all.

A Salopian by birth, after a short stay at Bradford Foulke retired to Blackpool where at 'one-penny-a-time', he would invite lads to take penalty kicks against him on the sands, offering a threepenny piece to successful candidates. Needless to say he was seldom out of pocket.

Willie died at the age of 40, from pneumonia. A remarkable man who also, briefly, played county cricket for Derbyshire, scoring one half-century and, not surprisingly, taking two catches, doubtless finding the small ball no problem to pouch in his large hands.

facts that I have laid before you, you will come to the conclusion that you really cannot refuse us!"

The votes were then counted. Leeds City (26), Burslem Port Vale (21) and Chelsea (20), narrowly ahead of Hull City (18) were elected. In the event, following further discussion, it had been decided to extend the League with the addition of four extra clubs, among them Clapton Orient.

There were now four clubs south of Birmingham (Woolwich Arsenal, Bristol City and Clapton Orient being the others) and the dominance of the North and the Midlands had been challenged. Be that as it may, all that mattered to the Chelsea directors and, of course, Frederick Parker who, most surprisingly, was not elected to the board until two years later, was that against all odds, Chelsea had won their first victory, and without a ball being kicked!

Off the field Chelsea's line-up had proved itself to be a match for the best in the land. Now, of course, even sterner battles lay ahead.

On Friday, 1 September 1905 at 6.05pm, the Manchester express steamed out of Euston on time, with the Chelsea FC team on board *en route* for their first-ever League fixture at Stockport. The Chelsea party stayed at the Albion Hotel, Manchester, and the game had inevitably aroused enormous interest locally.

Next day a brass band marched through the streets of Stockport followed by a goodly number of home-team supporters waving red and white scarfs. On alighting from the team bus, one four-foot urchin, totally unimpressed by Willie Foulke's towering presence, greeted him with, "Eh, ye'll get licked today, mister." Quick as a flash the goalkeeper replied, "It'll be the first time this year then mi lad!"

The Edgeley Park ground presented a strange backcloth for the occasion. It was reputedly 'the worst in the League' and a low, steep bank bordered close on one touch-line and behind a goal. There were two cart ruts crossing the playing area and one writer described it as 'an almost unbroken expanse of ripe plantation weed in full seed'.

In an even first half, little Martin Moran constantly threatened the Stockport goal, despite being several times dumped unceremoniously on to the perimeter banking, and Foulke was rarely called upon. It was after half-time that the fatal blow was struck and, according to a contemporary report, in somewhat unusual circumstances. A Stockport attacker was tripped on the penalty line and a spot kick awarded. Willie Foulke saved the shot at full stretch and threw the ball out to a colleague. The report continued: 'It pitched on to one of the numerous lumps and deviated sharply to the right. Foulke took the only course open to him and charged from his goal, but Stockport inside-forward, George Dodd, reached the ball first banging it straight at Marshall McEwan, who would have cleared it easily but for the fact that Tommy Miller was knocked into him by a County forward at the same time, and as a result the ball glanced off McEwan's chest into the net.' A classic case, one would think, for numerous television replays and a 'what happened next' slot for *A Question of Sport*.

The same writer thereupon concluded: 'Aided by their ground (which certainly wants 'knowing'), it will be a good team, and a lucky one, which brings points away from the Edgeley enclosure.'

At least the Chelsea bandwagon was rolling, and happier days lay ahead.

Promotion, Relegation And Promotion On The See-Saw

WITH the wealth and depth of talent available to Jock Robertson it was immediately clear that Chelsea would have no difficulty in holding their own in League football.

A strong squad had been assembled, even if little thought had been given to tactical planning. Rather the manager allowed individual talent to blossom and have free rein.

Seven days after the Stockport curtain-raiser, the player-manager himself scored Chelsea's first League goal in a 1-0 victory at Blackpool. Forty-eight hours later, in the very first competitive home fixture, a 6,000 crowd saw Jimmy Windridge notch a hat-trick and David Copeland score twice to send Hull City back to Humberside empty-handed.

Other good days followed swiftly. An impressive spell brought 11 points from six games and a position of third in the table was steadfastly maintained for the rest of the season with a consistency remarkable, and not too often achieved in subsequent years. The narrow gap between Chelsea and the top clubs Manchester United and Bristol City, however, proved insurmountable and promotion was never a likely outcome of an outstanding start.

But the crowds flocked into Stamford Bridge – over a quarter a million of them – with 67,000 attending the Good Friday fixture with Manchester United, a 1-1 draw. Outside London, too, several clubs clocked up their highest crowd of the season for the visit of Chelsea. Any doubts harboured by Gus Mears had been dispelled; Frederick Parker's faith and enthusiasm wholly justified. One unique event is worth chronicling. All Second Division clubs were given exemption from the qualifying rounds of the FA Cup competition. Chelsea, as a result of their late election to the Football League, however, were forced to come in at the beginning. Fortunately, the first two Cup-ties did not clash with League fixtures but, the third preliminary round, an away tie with Crystal Palace coincided with the Second Division home match against Burnley. Chelsea were ordered by the Football League to play their recognised first team, leaving the reserves to do battle with Palace. Not surprisingly they lost by a margin of 7-1 – and this having drafted in two players whose registration was, at best, doubtful.

As a result, the Football Association passed a resolution insisting the clubs must field full-strength teams in all matches in the knock-out competition.

For the 1906-07 season several new players were recruited. Willie Foulke had returned to Yorkshire to be replaced by Bob ('Pom Pom') Whiting, so named because of the immense length of his goal-kicks. And from West Ham United came George Hilsdon to replace, controversially, George Pearson scorer of 18 goals the previous year.

The 19-year-old recruit, however, wasted no time in silencing the critics by starting his Chelsea career with five goals in the opening match against Glossop. To this day this has not been bettered in a League match by any Chelsea player, and on only one occasion in an FA Cup match, in the following season when Hilsdon went one better and scored six times against Worksop. Meanwhile, he finished the season with 27 goals, as well as a hat-trick for the Football League against the Irish League.

The Chelsea team standing in the northern goal at Stamford Bridge. From left to right are: Watson, McRoberts, Key, Windridge, Mackie, Foulke, Copeland, J.T.Robertson, McEwan, Moran and Kirwan.

Chelsea on the attack against West Bromwich Albion at Stamford Bridge on 23 September 1905, Chelsea's second-ever home game. They won 1-0 with a goal from McRoberts in front of 20,000 fans.

Most important was the fact that Chelsea fulfilled their promising start of the first season by storming their way to promotion, finishing runners-up to Nottingham Forest and nine points ahead of Leicester Fosse, in third position.

In fact, for much of the time Chelsea led the field. With 16 wins and only three defeats from the first 22 League games they established a position of strength and never remotely looked like faltering. Apart from Whiting and Hilsdon, other signings, too, made their mark. Scottish international wing-half George Henderson came from Glasgow Rangers, defenders Joe Walton (New Brompton) and Ted Birnie (Crystal Palace) bolstered the meanest defence in the division, while Billy Bridgeman began his long career at Stamford Bridge. A dashing winger, he was to serve the club loyally for the next nine seasons.

Only one event marred the season. Jimmy Miller, Chelsea's first-ever trainer, died at Christmas. A former Scottish international, he was greatly respected by the players and to help his wife and two children, the famous comedian George Robey raised a team including the famous Welsh international winger, Billy Meredith, to play Chelsea the following April. George Robey himself also turned out, scored a brilliant goal, and subsequently signed amateur forms for the club.

So began Chelsea's music-hall connection which brought many stage stars flocking to Stamford Bridge and using the club's penchant for unpredictability as a source of material, not always welcome, for their stage scripts.

Life in the top division was never going to be easy in 1907-08, and so it turned out. Jock Robertson, his job well done, had left the previous October, with secretary William Lewis in temporary control. Now came David Calderhead, destined to be the club's longest-serving manager, a distinguished centre-half in his playing days, from Lincoln City. The annual injection of new players brought goalkeeper Jack Whitley, who was to serve the club for 32 years as player and trainer, and forwards Billy

New Chelsea manager David Calderhead, destined to become the club's longest-serving boss after he joined them from Lincoln City in August 1907.

Brawn, Percy Humphreys and Fred Rouse (Chelsea's first four-figure signing).

Starting with three defeats, and only three points from the first eight games, a final position of 13th was better than seemed likely for most of the time. Again, George Hilsdon was quite outstanding. Thirty goals

Chelsea hammer non-League Worksop Town 9-1 in the 1907-08 FA Cup. Above: Windridge scores for Chelsea.
Below: Chelsea force yet another corner.

from 35 League and FA Cup games undoubtedly kept Chelsea afloat, along with the regular contributions from his able lieutenant, Jimmy Windridge.

Certainly from the financial point of view, promotion paid off handsomely with total home attendance figures almost doubling to 625,000 and averaging nearly 33,000 per game. But Chelsea were running ahead of their time, and real capability, too quickly.

Hopes that firmer foundations for success in the top class had been laid were raised in the 1908-09 season. Of the newcomers, the most notable was Ben Warren, a fine wing-half from Derby County, already an England international, who won three more caps in his first year at Stamford Bridge. Tragically his days in London were to be numbered for he was all too soon to be struck down by illness which ultimately led to his early death at the age of 38.

Once more Hilsdon's scoring ability shone like a beacon light, this time 25 League goals from a somewhat meagre overall total of 56. This was largely responsible for Chelsea finishing two places higher in final table, 11th.

But any indication that they were now coming to grips with the greater challenge, proved misleading.

Sheffield Wednesday goalkeeper Lyall punches clear from a Chelsea attack at Stamford Bridge in October 1908.

Chelsea come close against Sunderland at Stamford Bridge in March 1910, but the game ended in a 4-1 defeat for the Londoners. At the end of the season Chelsea were relegated. Two points would have saved them.

Relegation clouds hovered over the club for most of the 1909-10 season even though it took a 2-1 defeat in the final game against Tottenham Hotspur at White Hart Lane to seal their fate, the crucial goal being scored by Percy Humphreys, who had left Stamford Bridge to sign for Spurs four months earlier.

At least Chelsea could point to a generous ration of ill-fortune. Hilsdon, injured in the second fixture, was missing for four months and managed only three goals. No fewer than 34 players turned out and various combinations and new faces were put on trial. Of these Sam Downing and, more notably, Vivian Woodward were to make the greatest impact. Downing an artistic, wing-half, was renowned for both his skill and scrupulous fair play. Woodward was already famous as the finest amateur centre-forward in the land and started a love affair with Chelsea which, as player and director, was to last for 21 years. But even his flair and genius could not prevent the return to the lower division.

Not that it was readily accepted. In the last two weeks the directors paid out £3,300 for three new players, Marshall McEwan, English McConnell, and Bob Whittingham, only the last of whom was to figure prominently in the Chelsea story.

If these panic measures had no immediate impact so far as staving off relegation was concerned, they did at least have one far-reaching effect. The Football League framed a new Rule (No.59) stating that: "After 5pm on the fourth Thursday in March in each season registrations, and transfers of registrations, may be declined or will only be approved subject to such limitations and restrictions as the Management Committee may determine, and if so determined, the Player shall only be eligible to play in the League matches for which permission is granted by the Management Committee." All three newcomers appeared in that last fixture – but to no avail.

So, the clock was turned back and the struggle for promotion began again. In many ways history repeated itself. As before, in 1910-11 third was Chelsea's position but, while four years previously it always seemed unlikely that they could close the gap between third and second places, this time they were in touch with the leaders from the turn of the year. In fact, having climbed into second spot in the table

after beating Leicester Fosse on 21 January, they doggedly clung on until the visit to Burnden Park on 26 April to meet leaders, Bolton Wanderers.

Unfortunately, three regulars were absent, right-back Walter Bettridge, who served the club so well in that position for 11 years being one of them. In front of a 36,000 crowd, Bolton won 2-0 and, in the final fixture, Gainsborough Trinity, then in 18th position, settled matters by beating Chelsea 3-1.

The basis of a successful team was, however, being built. Jim Molyneux was one of the most respected goalkeepers of the day. 'Jock' Cameron and Bettridge stalwart full-backs, Warren and Downing were established at wing-half and Whittingham, with 30 goals from inside-forward, and Hilsdon, scoring 18 times, gave Chelsea the strongest strike-force in the division. And, this time there was a new bonus.

For the first time Chelsea made their mark in the FA Cup competition, their five previous attempts having failed to survive the second round.

A goalless home draw against Southern League Leyton was hardly an auspicious start but comfortable wins in the replay and against Chesterfield Town, who had dropped out of the League the previous season, set up a visit to the Wolves' lair at Molineux, almost as daunting a prospect then as in the 1950s. "Never have I seen a more wonderful Cup-tie," crooned the programme editor seven days later. "My mouth was parched. My life was lit and relit a hundred times in forty-five minutes. I could not sit still." Vivian Woodward scored after a movement initiated by Hilsdon, and carried on by Charlie Freeman, with Hilsdon adding the second soon afterwards with a brilliant individual effort. Outclassed in the second half, it was the Chelsea defence which carried the day after half-time. "Never have players had to stand such buffetings as did the Pensioners on this occasion but not a man showed the white feather."

Chelsea in 1910-11. Back row (left to right): J.Moir (assistant trainer), E.McConnell, E.Jones, A.Douglas, -, J.Molyneux, H.Dolby, R.McRoberts, F.Taylor, A.Cousins, J.Walton, Vivian Woodward. Second row: A.Harding, R.Whittingham, G.Hilsdon, A.Wileman, G.Horn, J.Whitley, E.Bowles, H.Wileman, P.Smith, W.Bridgeman, H.Kane, J.Clark (head groundsman), H.Ranson (trainer), D.Calderhead junior. Seated: D.Calderhead senior (secretary-manager), Messrs G.Schonberg, H.Boyer, T.L.Kinton, J.H.Maltby, W.Claude Kirby (chairman), H.A.Mears, J.T.Mears, F.W.Parker (all directors), J.H.Palmer (reserve-team manager), A.J.Palmer (assistant secretary). Front row: N.Fairgray, A.Ormiston, B.Warren, C.Freeman, S.Downing, J.Windridge (captain), W.Cartwright, M.McEwan, J.Cameron, W.Brawn, W.Bettridge, K.McKenzie.

Next time out Swindon Town, beaten 3-1 at Stamford Bridge before 77,952 spectators, the largest number to assemble at the ground up to that time, proved less of an obstacle and a relatively easy passport to the semi-final against Newcastle United in Birmingham. Then, inevitably, class told and the Geordies won comfortably enough by three clear goals. But at least Chelsea had made their presence felt in knock-out football.

Just over 12 months later, in April 1912, there was greater cause for celebration. Chelsea were back in the First Division having finished in second place, level on goal-average with champions Derby County. It had been a long struggle and, although in touch with the leaders throughout the eight-month season, again it went to the final game, now against Bradford, at Stamford Bridge.

Not only had Chelsea to win, but Burnley, with superior goal-average, had at least to drop a point in their final fixture, at Wolverhampton.

Chelsea were foot-weary after their third game in six days but Charlie Freeman's goal after half-an-hour was enough to keep their hopes alive, although it still meant an agonising wait until news of Wolves' victory was relayed to an excited, waiting throng some 40,000 strong.

Whittingham had now taken over the goalscorer's mantle (26 goals), with Hilsdon absent through injury for much of the time. Woodward's great skill and artistry was a vital ingredient, despite not being regularly available, and Jack Harrow had arrived to start his long and distinguished career, beginning at left-half before moving to full-back.

Survival in Division One in 1912-13, proved just as uphill a task as it had been previously. Five successive defeats in October and November plunged the Pensioners into the danger zone from which they rarely struggled clear, even if this time it did not go to the final game. With Chelsea and Notts County battling it out for who should accompany Woolwich Arsenal out of the First Division, consecutive wins over Tottenham Hotspur and Middlesbrough (3-0 on Teesside) at least meant that the final game – against Notts County – held no terrors.

By now Hilsdon had returned to West Ham United, Whittingham was missing for much of the season with injury and Woodward shouldered an even bigger responsibility in the front line with Harry Ford and Billy Bridgeman lively attacking wingers.

For most of their eight seasons Chelsea had been

Chelsea on the attack against Liverpool at Stamford Bridge in September 1912, on their first season back in Division One. It was their first home game of the season and they lost 2-1 in front of 25,000 spectators.

George Hilsdon – Chelsea's Gatling Gunner

Few English football clubs can lay greater claim to having a distinguished, or more established line of centre-forwards than Chelsea. First of these was George Hilsdon, who arrived at the beginning of the club's second season to make an immediate, and spectacular, impact by scoring five goals on his League debut.

Less well recorded are the circumstances which brought him to Stamford Bridge. Towards the end of the 1905-06 season, manager Jackie Robertson had been recommended to watch a certain West Ham United reserve player who was likely to be available for transfer.

Having arrived at Upton Park, his attention was immediately riveted on a 19-year-old East London boy from Bow. "I never even set my eyes on the player I went to see," said Robertson. "They were glued all the time on the inside-left. If I get him he'll be our centre forward next season," he prophesied. And he was, making that sensational start, against Glossop at Stamford Bridge.

Luck, it is said, plays a large part in football, and certainly on this occasion it did Chelsea an enormous favour. Hilsdon's forte was primarily his powerful shooting, his nickname 'Gatling Gun George' arising from the frequency with which he propelled the ball past opposing goalkeepers before they had time to move. With right foot, or left foot, it made no difference.

If his feats of scoring made him famous, he was by no means merely a goal-machine. He had a wonderful positional sense, with a gift of stealing into open spaces to elude his marker. Immensely strong, with broad shoulders and thick thighs, he could hold his own physically with the strongest centre-halves, usually winning tackles and disdainfully brushing aside bulky opponents.

Strangely, West Ham had been slow to perceive such obvious potential and he made the promotion from reserve to first-team football naturally and without difficulty.

Within six weeks of his arrival at Chelsea he had been selected for the Football League XI to play against the Irish League, marking his representative debut with a hat-trick. International caps, eight of them in days of fewer such fixtures and in the face of stiff competition, followed as he became the best centre-forward in England.

For his first three seasons at Chelsea, nothing could stop his progress. 99 appearances. 76 goals, the majority in Division One, the club's promotion in 1907 being, not least, due to his deadly marksmanship. Injury in 1909-10 restricted him to a handful of games but he was back on song 12 months later.

Sadly, however, his last days at The Bridge became clouded in controversy. 'Too sociable. Too careless with his strength and vitality', it was said and so, in the summer of 1912, he returned to his alma mater in the East End.

Back in familiar surroundings, he banged in a further two dozen goals for the Hammers without ever quite recapturing his earlier flair and greatness, and the war, during which he was badly affected by mustard gas poisoning, effectively ended his career.

He died in 1941 at the comparatively early age of 56, but until recently his memory was commemorated by the weather-vane on the roof of Chelsea's West Stand on which the silhouette of the footballer was modelled on George. No doubt it will be relocated when the development of Stamford Bridge is completed.

Four days after the opening of the 1913–14 season, Chelsea's amateur goalkeeper R.G.Brebner, a dental surgeon by profession, tips the ball over from a Sheffield United attack at Stamford Bridge. Chelsea went on to win 4–2 before 40,000 with a hat-trick from Vivian Woodward.

Chelsea goalkeeper Jim Molyneux looks anxious as the ball goes narrowly wide against Spurs at Stamford Bridge on the opening day of the 1913–14 season.

A Bradford City forward is airborne at The Bridge in November 1913. Woodward's two goals earned Chelsea a 2-1 win.

March 1914 and Jim Molyneux scampers across his goal as Owen Marshall checks the on-rushing Sheffield United forwards. Chelsea won 2-0.

involved in struggles of one type or another to the end of their campaigns. Promotion twice. Relegation once. And at other times, various tense situations near one or other end of the table.

The 1913-14 season was one of relative comfort. Of consolidation, little excitement, maybe, but a mid-table

eighth place in the First Division was the best so far. Defeat at the hands of Millwall in the Cup was disappointing, this in a replay at home. More important, though, was an inflow of new players.

Harold Halse, England international, had already won a championship medal and two FA Cup winners'

Above: Harold Halse braves a flying Sunderland boot to head Chelsea's goal in the 1-1 draw against the Wearsiders at Stamford Bridge in December 1913.

Left: Chelsea's defence can do nothing to prevent Aston Villa scoring their second goal at Stamford Bridge in February 1914. Chelsea went down 3-0.

shirt, he was the epitome of the true amateur, never even claiming his expenses. Also, on three occasions towards the end of that season, Max Woosnam appeared at left-half. Like Woodward a true Corinthian, he was the outstanding athlete of his day. Subsequently playing also for Manchester City, he won four 'Blues' at Cambridge, represented Great Britain at lawn tennis in the Davis Cup, and England on the football field at both professional and amateur level. Sadly, business interests took him to Lancashire and his Chelsea connection was necessarily all-too-brief.

medals with Manchester United and Aston Villa. Of slight build he was an artistic inside-forward and a strong finisher. In contrast Tom Logan was a solid centre-half, but one who liked nothing better than to forsake defensive duties and lend support in attack. And then there was the 'Great Dane', Nils Middelboe, who graced the Chelsea scene for ten years, albeit somewhat irregularly. One of the most popular men to don the blue

At last Chelsea's future seemed assured but when the 1914–15 season began, so too had World War One.

The Khaki Cup Final

'THE Football Season of 1914-15 has opened under the shadow of the greatest and most momentous war in the history of the world.' So began the editorial introduction in Chelsea's first official programme of that autumn. Perhaps, moved by conscience and increasing public criticism, with Lord Kitchener mounting an appeal for half a million recruits to come forward, it continued: 'They will be forthcoming from no section of the community more readily than the maligned football player and follower.'

Surprisingly, the season was to run its full course, even in an atmosphere of increasing unreality and national unease, as well as dwindling attendances.

From the beginning, Chelsea once more floundered in the lower reaches of the First Division table. Vivian Woodward and Bob Whittingham had gone off to serve their country in different capacities, but there were no other departures of note and a considerable sum of money had been spent on a new left-wing pairing of Jimmy Croal (Falkirk) and Bobby McNeil (Hamilton Academicals, as they were then known), who together had represented the Scottish League the previous season. A third Scot to arrive was Laurence Abrams, from Heart of Midlothian, 'the best wing-half north of the border'.

However, only one victory was recorded before the middle of November. Another forward, Bob Thomson from Croydon Common, was also drafted in with some success, and this despite the handicap of having one eye. "How d'you manage?" he was once asked. "When the ball comes along," he replied. "I shut the other eye and play from memory."

From such an undistinguished start, Chelsea's League season never recovered. Off the field criticism that football was being played at all increased as the season wore on. On occasions demonstrations took place, although the 17th Middlesex Regiment, known as the Footballers' Battalion, recruited over 100 of the game's professionals among them Lieutenant V.J.Woodward. Grim reminders of what was happening on the other side of the Channel included letters in the Chelsea programme from soldiers in the trenches, and from a prisoner-of-war.

All was not despondency, however, and much-needed relief came from the FA Cup competition. Chelsea's first opponents were Swindon Town, Southern League champions the previous season, with the 'Moonrakers' opting to forego home advantage to play the fixture at Stamford Bridge. New emergency regulations were also in force. All Cup-ties were to be played on Saturdays and extra-time played at the first meeting.

Swindon drew the tie 1-1 with Chelsea winning the replay (also at The Bridge), 5-2 a week later, with outside-right Harry Ford the tallest member of the forward line at 5ft 7½ inches, and centre-half Tom Logan, 5ft 11in, the 'giant' of what must have been Chelsea's smallest-ever and most lightweight team.

Arsenal, installed in their new Highbury head-quarters after the move from Plumstead, were beaten in the second round by a goal from Halse. After the display against Swindon, this was 'good wine instead of water', said a writer who also reported on the Footballers' Battalion's march around the track at half-time, led by their brass band to resounding cheers of a 40,000 crowd, many themselves in khaki.

As a result, Chelsea were now London's last representatives in the FA Cup. Drawn against Manchester City (in second place in the First Division at the time) at Hyde Road was a tough assignment in the third round. But the Pensioners' first away win of the season could not have come at a more opportune moment. Clearly Thomson's 'memory' did not let him down on this occasion, for it was he who scored the only goal of the match. And the win appears to have surprised the team as much as the fans. On the journey up, McNeil had announced, "If we win we'll set the train on fire coming home." "If you do, they'll put it out and you too," was goalkeeper Jim Molyneux's sardonic reply. "Then, we'll no try; I'm no hand at walking a hundred miles," retorted the midget Scottish winger.

Newcastle United were Chelsea's fourth-round opponents at home and a 1-1 draw seemed to have ended any likely chance of further progress. But, again with extra-time being required, it was Harry Ford who scored the vital goal on Tyneside. One supporter recalls waiting at Stamford Bridge for the result to come through after the reserve fixture had ended. Assembled around the old creeper-clad office, a large crowd waited anxiously for over half an hour. With face pressed against the window he recalled the printing machine whirring laboriously and tapping out the letters, and the figure 'O' after the home team's name, to create an excitement which was drowned by the roar that greeted the '1' after Chelsea's name.

By now, Chelsea, with games in hand, were propping up all other teams in the First Division table as the first three months of the year brought a single win, five draws and three defeats.

But still the momentum was maintained in the knock-out competition. Mighty Everton, among the leaders in the championship race, were the opposition in the semi-final, and the venue Villa Park. And once again the form-book was overturned with goals from

Above: Chelsea skipper Jack Harrow meets his Sheffield United counterpart before the start of the 1915 FA Cup Final at Old Trafford.

Left: Soldiers watch the 1915 FA Cup Final between Chelsea and Sheffield United, giving the game the title of 'The Khaki Cup Final.

Croal and Halse, a brilliant individual effort this, giving Chelsea a well-deserved victory, which would have been more emphatic had not the same player lost his footing when clean through with only the goalkeeper to beat. And judging from the large number of letters received from soldiers and sailors serving their country overseas, the victory had raised morale both on foreign soil and on the high seas.

The Cup story, however was to have no happy ending. To minimise absenteeism from essential war work, the Final was switched from the Crystal Palace to Old Trafford, Manchester, much to Chelsea's disadvantage. The railway companies could provide only two trains, at full fare only, with 5s (25p) stand seats on general sale from the club offices to all-comers.

Meanwhile, the supporters of Final opponents, Sheffield United, had an easy journey (some 30 miles), and the ground was a mixture of red and white rosettes and khaki uniforms – the 'Khaki Final' as it became known – with scarcely a blue favour visible. The damp, murky atmosphere merely added to the general gloom that enveloped Chelsea increasingly as the day progressed.

From the moment the match began it was clear that Sheffield's half-back line would dominate the proceedings and the longer it continued the more depressingly one-sided things became, even if Chelsea limited the Blades to a single strike until six minutes from the end, when they added a further two goals. As the leading football writer of the day put it: 'Chelsea were as hapless as a reed shaken in the wind. They would not have scored had they played for a week.'

Jack Harrow
– Thou Good and Faithful Servant

BY THE very nature of their profession and the structure of the game, most players remain on stage for a comparatively brief span, before moving on to another club, or leaving the scene altogether.

A notable exception was Jack Harrow whose service to Chelsea covered a quarter of a century, as player and member of the training staff. Stamford Bridge has seen few more faithful servants down the years.

He first arrived in March 1911 for a modest £50 fee from the, then, fertile source of soccer talent, Croydon Common FC. Standing just under 5ft 8in, Harrow was small for a full-back but he compensated for any physical disadvantage by speed, of thought as well as of movement, and an inborn positional sense.

As a lad he had set his heart on being a centre-forward since he had already caught the eye with goalscoring feats in junior football, but he was switched to wing-half in emergency and it was while playing in that position that he was spotted, and signed, by Chelsea.

Almost immediately he had taken another step backward, in the positional sense, first to right-back, and then on to the opposite flank where he remained for the rest of his career.

When World War One started, he was 27 and an established first-team player. Joining the Royal Flying Corps he continued to turn out in wartime football, usually under his own name, but occasionally as 'De Haviland', on those occasions when he had escaped from camp without his CO's permission. Once, in fact, a writer commented on the Chelsea full-back who 'bore an uncanny resemblance to Jack Harrow'. Even loyalty to king and country took second place to Chelsea at times for Jack.

Another of his assets was his kicking, noted for its accuracy and power. Most of his 34 goals were scored from the penalty spot, or from free-kicks.

His career was played under the old offside law and his opinions on the new legislation make interesting reading."The new law killed full-back play. In my day there was a certain amount of art in our game. One full-back covered the other. Now the left-back covers one attacking flank and the right-back covers the other with neither venturing up to the halfway line". One suspects, therefore, that he would have approved of some of today's tactics which allow such freedom and aggression to enter into the role of the modern full-back.

In December 1924, and in the autumn of his career, Jack suffered damage to an eye when an opponent kicked a ball into his face from close range. "I could not judge the ball so well, or keep my eye on it so closely after that," he said, although he gamely carried on playing for another two years, past his 37th birthday.

Two England caps and an appearance for the Football League representative XI speaks well of his genuine pedigree as a player. Captain for much of his time at Chelsea, he remained on the training staff until the spring of 1938 when at last he bowed out gracefully.

The first player to chalk up more than 300 first-team games in a blue shirt, he was the ideal 'club-man'. An eagle-eyed Chelsea supporter visiting a relative in hospital years later spotted Jack Harrow in the adjoining bed. Jack was delighted at being recognised and the two were soon locked in conversation about 'the old days', the object of the man's visit taking second place to the distinguished patient in the next bed.

Up to the morning of the match, doubts surrounded the fitness of Harrow, Halse and Thomson. Vivian Woodward, home on military leave from France, had played in the two previous League games but emphatically stated that he would turn out only if Thomson, who had played in all the previous rounds, was unfit. Maybe he was also mindful of the morality of even the FA Cup Final being staged that season? For as Lord Derby, presenting the Cup and medals at the conclusion of the game summed up, "You have played well with and against one another. Play with one another for England now."

Four days later the curtain descended on Chelsea's first decade as a football club with a 2-0 defeat by Notts County, leaving them in last but one place in the table and, seemingly, back to Division Two. But fate was to intervene before normal football resumed four years on.

Meanwhile, for the remaining wartime seasons, in common with most League clubs, Chelsea soldiered on in regional football. A London Combination operated from September 1915 for four years, to continue as a competition for reserve teams after the cessation of hostilities.

In 1915-16 Chelsea won both the main and supplementary leagues aided by an influx of 'guest' players, among them Charles Buchan, then of Sunderland but later to become one of football's all-time star players, with Arsenal. He scored 40 goals that season, averaging well over a goal per game. The title was won again two seasons later and, in 1918-19, the London Victory Cup resided in Stamford Bridge trophy cabinet after Chelsea won the Final by three clear goals against Fulham at Highbury.

While Bob Thomson was chalking up a century of goals in those four seasons, an achievement equalled by Joe Payne a quarter of a century later in World War Two, others were engaged in different fields. Captain V.J.Woodward was wounded in action in January 1916, Tom Logan was awarded the Military Medal as was Arthur Wileman who was subsequently killed on active service. More than a dozen others of the club's professional staff were also in uniform overseas.

Hope And Despair Once Again

BEFORE normal League football could resume in September 1919, with Chelsea facing the unwelcome prospect of returning to sample Second Division fare once again, events off the field at the Lytham headquarters of the Football League, made the sporting headlines.

First, came the decision to extend by two the number of clubs in the First Division. And, secondly, an enquiry into a match between Manchester United and Liverpool in 1915 proved that the game had been 'arranged' to beat bookmakers operating fixed odds betting. This result influenced the final placings of both Manchester United (18th in the table) and Chelsea (19th) who were therefore due to be relegated. After various options had been aired, the upshot of all this was that Chelsea became reinstated in the First Division, with Arsenal being given an extra promotion place to make the second club in the enlarged section.

Victories from the first two fixtures sent Chelsea away to the best possible start. Fortunately, all but three of the Cup Final side of 1915 were still available. Tom Logan was still on active service overseas, but returned in November; wing-half Fred Taylor had moved to Brentford and Bob Thomson was not available, while Vivian Woodward, (who, of course had not played in the Final) had retired from the professional game. Into the side came Harry Wilding, another awarded the Military Medal in the war, as a Grenadier Guardsman, and wing-half George Dale, from Kilmarnock, who had appeared as a 'guest player' for Chelsea in the Victory Final earlier in the year. Wilding, equally at home at either centre-half and centre-forward, was to serve the club with distinction and a commanding presence for almost ten years.

Putting the ball into the opponents net was Chelsea's problem. Whittingham soon returned to his birthplace in the Potteries and the lightweight pre-war forwards, if lacking nothing in their skilful and clever approach work, urgently needed a proven goalscorer. In October, for the sum of £2,500, came Jack Cock from Huddersfield Town, who were in dire financial difficulties at that time. Another of Chelsea's 'big star' personalities had arrived. Also a holder of the Military Medal, he was delighted to return to his native London (he had been born in Brentford), marking his debut with two goals in the home fixture against Bradford and ending his first season at Stamford Bridge with 26 from 30 games. A magnificent athlete, it is a matter of surprise that he

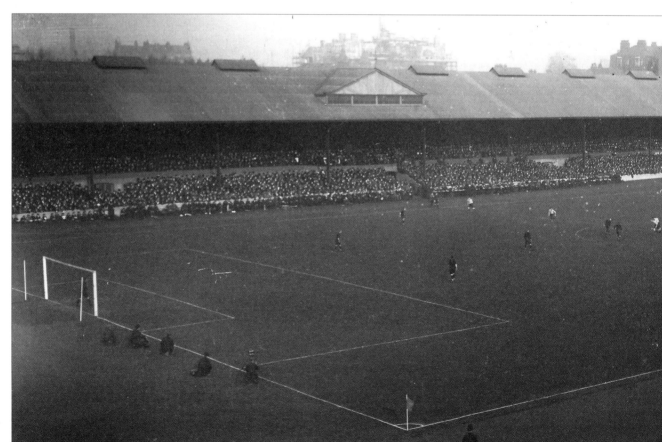

played only twice for England for whom he made his mark by scoring with virtually his first kick in international football.

Never seriously in contention for the championship, but maintaining a spot in the top six for most of the time, a final third place was easily Chelsea's best up to that time and, in fact, was not to be improved until their Golden Jubilee season 35 years later.

Further success, to underline Chelsea's progress and growing status in the game, came in the FA Cup. The four straight wins, with 12 goals scored and only one conceded, took them into the semi-final with a minimum of fuss. In fact, almost more publicity was given to the presence of His Majesty King George V at Stamford Bridge for the third round tie with Leicester City, and the King of Spain in the next, quarter-final, round against Bradford. A rumour that chairman Claude Kirby had been decorated by the Spanish monarch, delighted at the club's success, proved to be mischievous speculation.

Chelsea's passage into the last four in the competition now, however, raised a certain amount of discussion and argument.

Stamford Bridge had been selected as the venue for the 1920 FA Cup Final, yet the rules of the competition stated that the Final tie must be played on a neutral ground. Even so, it emerged that arrangements were so far advanced that it was too late to switch the game elsewhere.

Such worries were soon to be proved premature and irrelevant as Chelsea lost the semi-final tie, against Aston Villa at Bramall Lane, Sheffield, by three goals to one after a thoroughly disappointing display. That the League fixture against the same opposition, six days later, resulted in a 2-1 victory was scant consolation. Rather, solace was found in that, taking the season as a whole, it seemed Chelsea could now be counted among the country's top clubs. Never previously had a London team finished as high in the First Division, or amassed so many points (49).

But such optimistic thoughts proved to be sadly wide of the mark. Four years, totally lacking in distinction, were to follow, ending with a third relegation season in 1923-24.

New players were drafted in but mostly lacked the quality needed to build on existing foundations. Right-back Walter Bettridge's distinguished career at Chelsea ended in 1922, but Jack Harrow was to find a new and reliable full-back partner in George Smith, a Scotsman from Glasgow, who was to set a new record for the number of Chelsea first-team appearances. Tommy Meehan, a wing-half from Manchester United, was another excellent recruit, whose career was tragically terminated by his early death four years later. In addition, three outstanding amateurs threw in their lot with the club. But many others flitted briefly across the stage before disappearing from the scene altogether, having made little impression.

Nils Middelboe, who had played a handful of games before the war, returned to take over the captaincy, when available, and was a gifted half-back, having won 13 international caps for Denmark. For three seasons Dr John Bell performed with distinction and speed on the right wing while completing his medical studies in

Action at Stamford Bridge just after World War One when the ground was used to stage the FA Cup Final and other big games.

Action against Aston Villa at Stamford Bridge in September 1923. Top: Villa goalkeeper Cyril Spiers punches away from a Chelsea attack. Bottom: Jack Harrow lunges across to try to block a Villa shot as Chelsea goalkeeper Colin Hampton braces himself. Chelsea met Villa twice in eight days but both games were goalless. At the end of the season Chelsea dropped back to Division Two.

Jack Cock MM
– Soldier From The War Returning

When World War One began, Jack Cock was 19 and had just embarked on his career with Huddersfield Town, then a moderately successful Second Division team. A 'rookie' centre-forward of considerable potential.

During the four-year hiatus before normal peacetime soccer could resume, Jack returned to his native London, turning out in regional football for Brentford (where he began his professional career) and Croydon Common whenever his military duties allowed. Returning to Yorkshire in the autumn of 1919, it was to find his club in dire financial straits and, indeed, it was to keep Town in business that Chelsea paid £2,500 for his services that October, as well as solving their own problem in attack.

Bob Whittingham was no longer the force he had been, Vivian Woodward had retired, and Bob Thomson unable to score goals with the regularity of his earlier days.

Huddersfield's monetary troubles meant Chelsea had acquired not only a magnificent centre-forward but also a fine athlete, strong and perfectly proportioned.

Just before he arrived at Stamford Bridge, he had won his first England international cap and his impact on the team was immediate. Scoring twice on his debut against Bradford City, he was leading scorer by the end of that 1919-20 season, with 24 goals from 30 games.

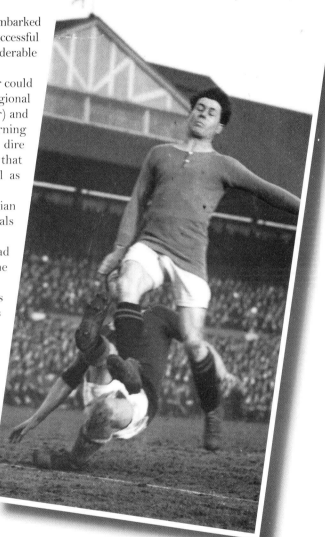

He was a glutton for work. Almost an over-conscientious trainer, Jack Whitley would constantly be damping his enthusiasm. "You've done enough for one day, Jack," he would say. But once Whitley's back was turned he would be back hard at it, sprinting and lapping round the old greyhound track.

A deadly marksman, as his 200 goals in senior football proves, he hit shots into the net from either foot with equal power and accuracy. His fine heading ability, too, brought him many goals.

In his first season with Chelsea he was an important member of the team which reached the FA Cup semi-final as well as achieving a place in the top three of the League Championship. But thereafter, strangely, Cock never quite maintained his excellent start. His output of goals fell away markedly during the next two seasons, good days being followed by longer spells of comparative indifference.

He was very much a man of moods. His display for England against Scotland in the Victory International at Sheffield in 1920, when he scored two of his country's goals on a waterlogged mud heap, was described by one writer as 'the best centre-forward exhibition ever', a level he could not sustain.

By the early months of 1923 much of his sparkle and enthusiasm seemed to have left him and he was transferred to Everton after which he moved, briefly, to Plymouth Argyle, before finishing his career on a high note with Millwall (92 goals in 135 appearances), and helping them to the Third Division title in 1928. From 1944 until 1948 he returned to manage the 'Lions' and was in charge when they met Chelsea in the wartime 1945 League South Cup Final at Wembley.

Football was Jack Cock's life for over 30 years. Blessed with the striking good looks of a film star, he possessed a fine tenor voice and, indeed, supplemented his football income, by appearing on the music-hall stage.

The final years of his life were spent in South London where he had been a publican in New Cross. He died in 1966 aged 72, still well recognised and a well-liked and popular figure.

London and subsequently turning professional. And the third unpaid player, the famous Corinthian Benjamin Howard Baker was first-choice goalkeeper for five seasons, whenever he could find time to turn out.

Such individual talent, however, did not produce sustained success on the field and was too frequently unavailable.

The 1920-21 season saw Chelsea propping up the other First Division clubs at the end of October and, although this was followed by three victories and a draw, the mere avoiding of relegation became their sole objective, which, in fact, was achieved comfortably enough in the end. Jack Cock's output of goals declined to 15 but he was still leading scorer with James Ferris, an Irishman from Belfast, his most able lieutenant.

In the FA Cup, three laboured attempts were required to remove both Reading and Plymouth Argyle from the competition. Swindon Town were other victims, but another semi-final appearance was thwarted by a single-goal defeat at the hands of Cardiff City at Ninian Park.

An indifferent start to the 1921-22 campaign suggested a further struggle to stay in the top class, when only four points separated Chelsea from the bottom club in the table in mid-January and the Pensioners had already been knocked out of the FA Cup at the first hurdle. However, the remaining 17 games brought seven consecutive victories (the best winning sequence up to that time) and only two defeats. Ninth was a creditable final position, but Chelsea were deservedly acquiring the reputation of the complete unpredictability that has been a feature of the club ever since. Cock's goals, only 13 this time, were crucial in a season when only Oldham Athletic had a worse output than Chelsea's meagre total of 40.

Thankfully, with Howard Baker, Harrow, Smith, Meehan and Wilding such solid defensive pillars, Chelsea's rearguard's record was bettered only by the champions, Liverpool, and runners-up, Tottenham Hotspur.

When a crowd of 40,000 assembled to welcome the 1922-23 campaign there were no new signings on parade. Four new players were on the pay-roll, three of them defenders and a third, Albert Thain, a scheming inside-forward.

Thain had learned his football with a railway works side and it was suggested that he signed for Chelsea because he would feel at home listening to main line and underground trains rumbling past Stamford Bridge. Certainly, for whatever reason, the place suited him. He wore the blue shirt for eight seasons and his long-striding runs frequently left opponents trailing helplessly in his wake.

Before the season descended into a fight to stay in the division, Chelsea at least managed one brief moment of glory. Having beaten Stoke on the evening of Monday, 4 September, for the first time they found themselves on top of the First Division. But as one writer warned: "The defeat inflicted on Stoke made the enthusiastic supporters look on the future through rose-tinted glasses… at the same time it would be unwise to chortle prematurely."

Whereupon things did start to go wrong. Injuries piled up, the most notable absentee being Cock who managed only one goal from 11 games, and there was no successor to the throne he had occupied with success for four years. Not a single goal was scored in November and the toothless Pensioners dropped rapidly down the table. By Easter, only four points separated Chelsea (20th) from the bottom club, whereupon, and against all reason and likelihood, the final seven fixtures brought a lone victory and six drawn games. By no means spectacular but least sufficient for survival.

But it had been an uphill struggle. League attendances at Stamford Bridge had fallen by nearly 200,000, the biggest crowd (67,105) watching a second round FA Cup-tie with Southampton. Even that failed to produce a spark, or even a goal, and the replay at The Dell was lost four days later.

Jack Cock had now transferred his skills to Everton and the yawning gap left behind, remained unfilled. The 1923-24 season not only inevitably brought relegation once more, but only 31 goals were scored over the eight-month long season. Winger Jackie Crawford and the versatile Harold Miller (already capped by England with Charlton Athletic) began their lengthy Stamford Bridge careers and a third acquisition arrived from Middlesbrough in November.

Andy Wilson was destined to become one of Chelsea's greatest stars and no more popular player ever donned the blue shirt. Already, possessing 12 Scottish caps, he was a true artist and wonderful old-fashioned 'dribbler'.

For £6,500 (a club record at that time), Chelsea may have seen him as Cock's successor, but Wilson was essentially a provider and was soon to move to inside-forward leaving others to reap the benefit of his skill, by putting the ball in the net.

Only eight goals had been scored from 17 games prior to Wilson's arrival and, not surprisingly, the Blues were already in serious trouble at the foot of the ladder.

And so it remained until, by the beginning of April, a five-point gap separated Chelsea (21st) from Preston North End above them, with only four games remaining.

A visit from League champions, Liverpool, scarcely seemed promising and the hard-pressed programme writer openly stated that 'the last hope was shattered at Newcastle,' where Chelsea had lost the previous week.

But, true to reputation, if not to form and logic, the tottering Pensioners won that game and also the remaining three fixtures. Too late. The gap was closed but Chelsea were still relegated by virtue of their indifferent goal-average. It had been calculated that seven or eight goals were needed in the final game against Manchester City. Almost unbelievably three of them came in the first quarter of an hour of that game, whereupon the heavens opened and the rains descended to turn the pitch into a morass. The midget Chelsea forwards faded away, almost sunk from view.

Some 40,000 fans, Chelsea's highest attendance for six months, went home drenched to the skin and well entertained to contemplate what might have been and to prepare, had they known it, for six seasons in Division Two.

The Long Road Back

BEFORE Chelsea had time to recover from the loss of First Division status and the financial debts incurred in the desperate effort to avoid their fate, notably through the signing of centre-forward Billy Brown from West Ham United for a sizable fee, another, and tragic, blow struck the club. Tommy Meehan died days before the start of the new 1924-25 season.

A stylish and constructive wing-half, a non-smoker and teetotaller, he was one of the most popular players of his day. Some 2,000 people paid tribute to this fine man at his funeral in Wandsworth, and a fund for his wife and children raised some £1,500 with contributions from at least 15 other League clubs. A benefit match against a representative Football League XI at Stamford Bridge was also played on behalf of the memorial fund.

There were no new signings destined to make a lasting impression, although one, centre-half Arthur Sales from Redhill Athletic, was supposedly the fastest footballer in the game, having covered 100 yards in 10.5 seconds. Soon, however, the tried and tested James Frew, or Wilding, were again the men in possession at the heart of the defence.

The goal famine was solved, temporarily at least, by Bill Whitton, who found Second Division defences a good deal easier to unlock, and 16 goals from 22 games was, surprisingly, the best ratio by any Chelsea forward for 11 years.

Howard Baker was regularly available in goal; Smith and Harrow generally considered to be the most reliable full-backs in that division, and Crawford and McNeill, after 11 seasons in a blue shirt, dangerous raiders down the flanks. And, of course, there was Wilson, in his first full season supplying craft and laying on a good supply of chances for Whitton, in particular, as well as scoring ten times himself.

Five consecutive draws in September and October just about left Chelsea in touch with the top clubs, but six defeats in seven games between February and early April prevented any chance of the gap being closed. A disappointing season included a first round exit from the FA Cup, against Birmingham at St Andrew's. Amazingly, the average home attendance was nearly 31,000, a tribute to the loyalty of the long-suffering supporters.

In 1925-26 a modification to offside law came into operation for the first time and Chelsea responded by scoring 11 goals in their opening two away fixtures. In the first home game the referee did not once have cause to blow his whistle for an offside infringement.

Whitton had now been replaced at centre-forward by Bob Turnbull, a Scot whose professional career was spent entirely in London, Arsenal, Charlton Athletic and Clapton Orient being his other clubs. Ten goals from his first six games of the season was too good to last, but at least it put Chelsea on top of

Chelsea pictured in 1924-25. Back row (left to right): A.Wilson, J.Priestley, P.McKenna, J.Frew, C.Hampton, D.Cameron, H.Ford, W.Morrison, H.Brown. Middle row: David Calderhead (manager), J.Fraser, H.Wilding, F.Barrett, J.Ashford, S.Plum, B.Duffy, G.Rodger, R.G.Jenkins, G.Smith, J.Whitley. Front row: J.Crawford, W.Whitton, W.Brown, A.Thain, J.Harrow, J.Armstrong, S.Castle, H.Miller, W.Ferguson, R.McNeil.

Scottish international Andy Wilson hangs a portrait of himself in his new London home after his £6,500 transfer to Chelsea in November 1923.

Amateur international goalkeeper B.Howard Baker punches clear clear from a Bradford City forward at Stamford Bridge on the opening day of the 1925-26 season. Another famous amateur, A.G.Bower, covers the goalmouth. Both amateurs also won full England caps.

the table. Defeat was not tasted until the second half of November when, deservedly on the day, Swansea Town at last lowered the blue flag.

More damaging was a pointless Christmas and New Year, knocking the Pensioners from their perch at the top of the table and putting them seven points adrift of leaders Derby County, a gap which was never closed. One reason was an injury to Andy Wilson, who played in only three games after the turn of the year, and which caused the supply of goals to dry up.

There had been few changes in personnel, Albert Thain played his first full season in the senior side and John Priestley and Willie Ferguson were stalwart wing-halves. Again, an infuriating inconsistency was responsible for many of the problems. Lowly Clapton Orient won comfortably at The Bridge, yet Derby

Fulham goalkeeper McKenna clears his lines at Stamford Bridge in September 1925, but Chelsea won 4-0 on their way to finishing third in Division Two.

County, on their way to promotion, were sent away empty-handed.

In the FA Cup, a record 41,000 filled Selhurst Park to see Third Division Crystal Palace win 2-1. At least it kept the music-hall artists well supplied with material even if it was not so appreciated by the Chelsea faithful at the front of the house.

And in many ways the 1926-27 season was to prove a carbon copy of its predecessor. Fast out of the traps, and leading the field in September, an indifferent spell up to Christmas had seemingly been repaired by seven consecutive League victories in February and March, although by that time Middlesbrough, the subsequent champions, had pulled away from the rest of the pack. But, it proved impossible to sustain this sequence into the final straight, the damage being typically inflicted by set-backs at Clapton Orient again, and Barnsley. Three points from the last five fixtures left Chelsea trailing in fourth position, five points adrift of promoted Derby County.

Still the faithful poured through the turnstiles, over 70,000 of them in a fifth round FA Cup tie, subsequently won by Cardiff City after a replay. And League 'gates' again averaged almost 30,000.

Prominent were three newcomers. Goalkeeper Simeon ('Sam') Millington came straight from non-League football in Shropshire to succeed Howard Baker, and his regular deputy Peter McKenna. For six seasons he guarded the Chelsea net with distinction, a cloth cap his badge of office. A supporter of those days recalls with amusement a goalmouth mêlée when Sam's cap became dislodged, and he was seen to

launch himself into a horizontal dive to reclaim his headgear, while his colleagues frantically concerned themselves with keeping the ball out of the net at the other end of the goal.

Also at this time, Tom Law, from Glasgow Waverley, made his debut and was to remain a familiar figure, as player and, latterly, spectator, for 50 years and virtually to the end of his life. Lacking a little pace, maybe, he nevertheless became one of the outstanding left-backs of his era and a member of Scotland's 1928 'Wembley Wizards'.

The third of the new trio was George Pearson who took over the left-wing berth from little Bobby McNeill, after his 12 years' loyal service, the last survivor of the 1915 FA Cup Final team. At 5ft 2ins, one of the smallest players to play for the club, his speed and thunderous shooting belied his tiny frame.

Consecutively finishing fifth, third and fourth in the table was frustrating enough. Yet, at their fourth attempt to get back to the First Division, Chelsea once more managed to miss the boat, this time by three points and a single place. Once more they topped the table for nearly three months up to Christmas, stringing together eight consecutive victories before fading after Easter, when another injury to Andy Wilson proved crucial.

Into the team came Jimmy Thompson, signed as a left winger from Luton Town, but converted to centre-forward so successfully that in 29 League games he scored 25 goals. Important though this contribution was at this time, it was 30 years later as a talent scout in the post-World War Two era that he made an even greater impact by unearthing a rich vein of schoolboy prodigies to make the Chelsea youth scheme the envy of every club in the country.

Apart from Thompson, the other arrival was Jack Townrow, also a Londoner, an England international centre-half renowned as one of the last 'attackers' in his position, before the introduction of the new offside law made such enterprising and entertaining players largely redundant.

But these infusions of new blood were not enough. A settled team was clearly the most talented in the Second Division, and the fact that two of the defeats in the final week of the season were at the hands of relegated South Shields and lowly Barnsley was all too typical.

Twelve months later, as the curtain came down on the 1928-29 season, feelings were little different. Chelsea were left to lick their wounds after finishing in the obscurity of a mid-table berth. Ninth in Division Two was to be their lowest placing in the first 70 years of the club.

For some reason never made clear, Thompson, after the impressive form of his first season, was relegated to the London Combination side and what was, then, the considerable sum of £3,600 was shelled out for Sid Elliott who had scored 26 times in his only season at Fulham, 12 months previously. But Stamford Bridge never witnessed any repetition of such deeds and when Thompson was belatedly recalled, on Boxing Day, he responded with a hat-trick, and went on to score eight goals in seven games before dropping out though injury and never playing for Chelsea again. Ironically, south of the river, Jack Cock continued to score goals prolifically with Millwall, chalking up his 250th in League football during that season.

It was all bitterly disappointing after starting the campaign with six consecutive wins. Thereafter points were, characteristically, needlessly lost to sides in the nether regions of the table. Outstanding individual talent, reinforced by the signing of the accomplished international wing-half Sid Bishop from West Ham United, could not be blended into a winning team. And, it must be admitted, several new signings failed to make any impression whatsoever.

Easily the most memorable event was the 2-0 defeat of Everton, described by one writer as 'possibly the richest football club in the land,' in the FA Cup before 61,000 customers at The Bridge. Townrow shackled the legendary 'Dixie' Dean, as Thompson and Harold Miller sneaked late goals at the other end. Birmingham were beaten in the following round, before Portsmouth, in a replay at Fratton Park, ended further progress, and ambition.

Loyalty was being strained to its limits as Chelsea's supporters continued to outnumber those of many clubs in the higher division. Not for the first time the cry that the club did not want promotion was raised on the flimsy grounds that a winning team in the Second Division was preferable to a struggling First Division side.

Disabled ex-servicemen watching a match at Stamford Bridge in February 1926. Eight years after the end of World War One, the dreadful consequences of the conflict were still all too obvious.

Chelsea goalkeeper 'Sam' Millington is beaten by a Wolves' shot at Molineux in January 1928 as Chelsea go out of the FA Cup at the first attempt. Millington was a key member of the Londoners' side which returned to Division One in 1930 but two years later was forced to retire because of illness.

Rather than licking their wounds, Chelsea then proceeded to set a new trend by spending several weeks on a summer tour in Argentina. Coincidentally or not, the change of environment brought about a change of fortune on their return. And, maybe, it was a positive factor in bringing about promotion ten months later.

"We really learned the meaning of team-work out there," said Andy Wilson. "And the fortnight's sea voyage on the way home set us up for the big effort." The team had performed impressively on that tour, too. Looking back it was the ideal preparation for launching a suitable celebration of the club's Silver Jubilee.

There were few new faces. George Rodger, not a newcomer, took over the centre-half position. Irishman Sam Irving shared the right-half spot with Scotsman Willy Russell in a side settled, apart from the 'problem' position of centre-forward.

By Christmas Chelsea were in sixth place when they received a valuable, and most urgently sought, present in the shape of a new leader of the attack. The name of G.R.Mills appeared in the programme team

Andy Wilson
– The Complete Craftsman

When World War Two broke out in 1939, Chelsea had completed 30 seasons of League football, their somewhat chequered career never reflecting the glittering array of talent the club had paraded in those years. At that juncture a popular vote from spectators who had supported the 'Pensioners' throughout that period would, almost without question, have placed Andy Wilson at the top of the list of those forwards who had played for the club up to that time.

Andy arrived at The Bridge in November 1923 from Middlesbrough, having led Scotland's attack in their 12 previous internationals, latterly as captain of his country. The fee of £6,500 almost a record at that time.

The scoring of goals was never his chief asset. He was a true artist, drawing opponents before taking them out of the game with a pass of pin-point accuracy, or leaving them foundering in his wake with his delicate footwork. As Fulham's Johnny Haynes was to do more than 30 years on, he could also open up opposing defences with long, sweeping, passes to the far wing.

With the change in the offside law, Wilson was, in fact, largely responsible for the general adoption of the 'W' formation, dictating the run of play as a deep-lying inside man behind his centre-forward and two wingers.

Football was in Wilson's blood having been reared in Lanarkshire. Once asked when he began to learn the game, he replied, "Only a wee while before I learned to walk."

His eight seasons in the Chelsea teams coincided with days of varying fortunes. Initially he was largely responsible for keeping the club in the First Division in his first season at The Bridge. Then, as captain, he led his side to promotion back into the top class in 1930 after several seasons of near-misses and agonising frustration. Appropriately, his final year was again spent where he belonged, amongst the best – and in the company of Hughie Gallacher, Chelsea's latest expensive Scottish recruit.

Life was not always easy for Andy, 5ft 6½in in height, strict dieting was necessary to keep his weight to around 12st. But his greatest handicap was an almost totally disabled left arm, a legacy of World War One, and a disability which he cast aside lightly.

He was more than just one of the finest footballers of his generation. He had a single-figure handicap at golf; he could make century breaks on the billiard table; and he was one of the outstanding bowls players in the country, proved by an ample collection of silverware trophies.

His football career wound down with a brief stay at Queen's Park Rangers and in French football, with Nîmes. Briefly, he tried his hand at management, with Walsall, before returning 'home' to settle in London for the rest of his life.

For 20 years after World War Two he was a regular resident in a seat in the old East Stand at The Bridge. Instantly recognisable, and warmly greeted by his many fans who had enjoyed and marvelled at his great skill. Briefly, his son, Jimmy, was on the club's staff in the 1950s.

Andy died in October 1973, aged 77, after a long and successful life. Enormously respected on the field, he was universally popular wherever he went.

Andy Wilson leads out Chelsea on the opening day of the 1928-29 season. Chelsea got off to a fine start, beating Swansea Town 4-0 in the Second Division. The following season Chelsea won promotion.

Chelsea's team which lost at The Hawthorns in October 1929. Back row (left to right): Irving, Smith, Higgs, Bishop, Law. Front row: Crawford, Wilson, Elliott, Miller, Pearson, Townrow. Goalkeeper Frank Higgs, standing in for the injured Millington, made only two senior appearances for Chelsea. Millington returned to help steer Chelsea back to Division One that season.

on 21 December against Preston as a virtual unknown. Chelsea had at last found the piece to complete their jigsaw.

Bernard Hugh, the artist responsible for the cartoon on the front page of the Official Programme for so many years, helped to introduce the raw, gangling recruit. "for the benefit of those thousands of supporters who stayed at home or went to Woolworth's matinees I give the following impressions of the Pensioners' great 5-0 victory over Preston North End on Saturday. Let me introduce G.R.Mills, the gentleman from Bromley. Our latest leader, he went over the top at 2.30, and at 2.32 dropped one of his bombs in the enemy's camp."

Soon the initials disappeared as he signed professional forms. By the end of April he had scored 14 goals, with Wilson and the left-wing pair of Miller and Pearson also reaching double figures. The goal 'famine' was over at long last. Chelsea scraped into second place to finish two points ahead of Oldham Athletic.

But the race was not decided until the final day, and then with high drama. Chelsea journeyed north to take on Bury at Gigg Lane needing a win to ensure promotion. If that match were lost, however, Oldham, playing at Barnsley, could leap-frog over the Pensioners provided they won.

Supported by a strong contingent of fans, many travelling on a 'special restaurant car' train at 16s (80p) per head, Chelsea did indeed lose, by a single goal, happily their disappointment immediately being dispelled with news that Oldham, too, had been defeated at Oakwell.

Six years of waiting were over. Some of the more faint-hearted had lost hope – Chelsea's home attendances had fallen to their lowest since the war. But for the faithful majority, their loyalty had been well-rewarded after so much patience and frustration.

The Glamour Days, But No Success

HAVING been thwarted in their attempts to get back to the First Division on six occasions, the board of directors immediately made it clear that they intended to spare no cost in maintaining Chelsea's hard won position.

Claude Kirby was still in control as chairman, J.T.Mears was another director who had served since the club's foundation, and David Calderhead was starting his 23rd season as secretary-manager. And all connected with the club were only too aware of what was happening a few miles away in North London as Herbert Chapman's Arsenal were also seen to be sparing no effort, or expense, both on and off the field, to make the Gunners the most successful, and most talked about, club in England.

From the start of 1930-31 season, Chelsea's policy was clear enough. Nothing would be withheld in order to strengthen the playing staff. What, more unfortunately, went overlooked was the fact that a large assembly of talent itself is no guarantee of success. Some of the star names converging on Stamford Bridge may have thrilled the large crowds in the decade leading up to World War Two, but there were too many temperamental prima donnas among them, and not all could resist the attractions of the glitter and glamour to be found in the capital, off the field.

Three Scotsmen led the parade. Hughie Gallacher was, at £10,000, to be the jewel in the crown. Alex Cheyne (£6,000) from Aberdeen, was also an established international. But even these two could not always outshine the 'Gay Cavalier', Alex Jackson, the dashing winger from Huddersfield Town. Yet, ironically, and perhaps not altogether surprisingly, it was George Barber, a sleek-haired tall full-back obtained from Luton Town on a free transfer who was to serve the Pensioners longer and more faithfully, than any of the big names.

With the tried and tested Sam Millington in goal, George Smith and Law at full-back, and half-backs Willie Russell, Sam Irving, Jack Townrow, George Rodger, Sid Bishop and Willie Ferguson available, there was stability enough in defence and indeed it was renowned as one of the meanest in the League. But even with the promptings of Andy Wilson, and the crafty wing-play of Jackie Crawford and George Pearson, the goals expected from Gallacher, Cheyne and Jackson never materialised. A total of 34 was a respectable tally, but scarcely good value for the money spent. A 6-2 victory in the first home fixture was to prove illusory. Only on 15 occasions thereafter was the ball placed in opponents' nets more than once during a match.

Consolidation in the top league was achieved easily enough, Chelsea hovering around the middle of the table throughout the season. Highlights were few. Gallacher's return to Tyneside attracted an attendance of 68,386 to see Newcastle United, his former employers, win by a single goal. Chelsea were picked out as a good bet for the Cup, but Birmingham

In 1930-31, back in Division One, Chelsea reached the quarter-finals of the FA Cup, where they lost to Birmingham in a second replay. Here in the third round at Upton Park, Hughie Gallacher attempts to lob the Hammers goalkeeper.

nevertheless won a sixth round replay, at the Bridge, 3-0. Statisticians noted that the 11 goals scored from the penalty spot was a new club record. Law (seven) and Leslie Odell (four), never a regular at full-back, were the marksmen.

Neither did matters improve in 1931-32. Indeed, by Christmas with Chelsea in 21st place, alarm bells were ringing. Four of the faithful old guard, Millington, George Smith, Townrow and Wilson played their last games for the club and Harold Miller and George Mills were recalled, a greater reliability than that of some of their more mercurial colleagues adding much-needed fibre to the team.

One other big signing arrived in November when Peter O'Dowd, a stylish and constructive centre-half, made his debut against Everton at Goodison Park. A 7-2 home win, with 'Dixie' Dean scoring five times was scarcely the most auspicious of starts but, although his time at Chelsea (just over two years) was brief, many who saw him insist that he has a strong claim to a place in any Blues team of all time.

Consolation at another merely ordinary League season came in the FA Cup. Tranmere Rovers (after a replay), West Ham United, Sheffield Wednesday (also at the second attempt) and Liverpool, at Anfield, were eliminated in turn. Chelsea were revelling in the big match atmospheres and 15 goals were scored as nearly a quarter of a million fans flocked through the turnstiles to see those games.

Huddersfield was the venue for the semi-final; Newcastle United the opposition. But two early goals from Gallacher's former team mates were to prove decisive, although Hughie, himself, did reduce the deficit. It was the Geordies' seventh win in eight semi-finals. One writer attributed their success to 'the tactical talks' said to have been a feature of their Cup preparations. One suspects that any such approach rarely featured very seriously on Chelsea's agenda in those days.

Nor was it to be a case of 'third time lucky' so far as 1932-33 was concerned. Chelsea's reputation for 'pretty' football once more attracted large crowds up and down the country, and individual skills prospered. But, in terms of results, it proved totally ineffective. Soon avoiding relegation once again became the dominant objective.

Another Scot, full-back Bob Macaulay, arrived but never adapted to the English game. Eric Oakton, a winger from Bristol Rovers and more of a journeyman, proved a better investment. In January Allan Craig, from Motherwell, was signed to shore up an ailing defence and made an immediate impact, first at wing-half and then centre-half.

Most notable of all, however, was a signing that cost the club the nominal £10 signing on fee. Vic Woodley, taking over from Millington (then aged 36) in goal, played in every match. At 21, and with playing experience limited to service with Windsor and Eton FC, he bridged the gap between the amateur and professional game with a minimum of fuss and, above all, brought reliability where and when it was most needed.

Even so, with ten games to play Chelsea were lodged in 21st place, having already been ignominiously knocked out of the Cup by Brighton and Hove Albion. After carelessly forgetting to claim exemption from the qualifying rounds, this was Albion's eighth tie in the competition, their passage having started at Shoreham and progressed to include victims such as Worthing, Hastings and St Leonard's, and Barnet among others. At least on this occasion music-hall comedians found an alternative source of mirth, with Walsall knocking out mighty Arsenal on the same afternoon. One Chelsea director, Colonel

George Mills scores Chelsea's winner in the home fourth-round tie against Arsenal.

Chelsea pressing on the Blackburn goal in the fifth-round tie at Stamford Bridge, where the Londoners won 3-0.

Chelsea goalkeeper 'Sam' Millington looks at the ball through the legs of fellow defender Peter O'Dowd. George Barber is also on the ground.
The opponents are Arsenal at Stamford Bridge in 1931-32.

Difficult to spot the Chelsea players because both sides had to wear change strips – and both chose stripes. One player who is obvious is Birmingham goalkeeper Harry Hibbs, struggling to reach the ball in the first game at St Andrew's. The Midlanders won 3-0 in the next game back at Stamford Bridge.

*Hughie Gallacher has his eyes shut but the Huddersfield defender
appears to be pulling his goalkeeper's cap down over his eyes! Chelsea
lost this game at Stamford Bridge 1-0 in January 1933.*

C.D.Crisp, was to become club chairman three years
later. Then Mayor of Lewes, nine miles away along
the road, he probably failed to see the humour of the
situation more than most.

Not until the final week of the season was Chelsea's
future in the First Division assured, by a 4-1 victory
against Manchester City at Maine Road, with
Gallacher scoring a hat-trick. Earlier had come the
announcement that Dave Calderhead was retiring
from his post after 26 years.

The 'Chelsea Sphinx' as he was known, was
certainly a man of action
rather than words. A Scottish centre-half, with one
international cap, he was
much respected, but an
essentially private man and
far removed from the image
of most of the managers of
today.

*Hughie Gallacher tries to
outjump West Ham's Chalkley
and Barrett during Chelsea's
3-1 FA Cup win in the fourth
round at Stamford Bridge in
January 1932. Chelsea
reached the semi-final that
year, where they lost 2-1 to
Newcastle at Huddersfield.*

Tommy Law
– Full-back Wizard

THE Chelsea careers of Andy Wilson and Tommy Law ran strangely parallel courses. Both were born and reared in Lanarkshire, represented their country and, having arrived in London to play for Chelsea, spent the rest of their lives within close range of Stamford Bridge.

One notable difference, however, was the fact that Law was plucked from Glasgow junior football, in which he had played only five games for the Waverley club, whereas Wilson had furthered his education with Heart of Midlothian, Dunfermline Athletic, and Middlesbrough, before arriving in the Fulham Road.

'Too Slow' was the cry from the pundits when first they saw the new recruit. And, indeed, he was certainly no greyhound. But, admittedly at a time when speed of thought rather than speed of foot was the order of the day, Law rapidly became recognised for what he was. One of the

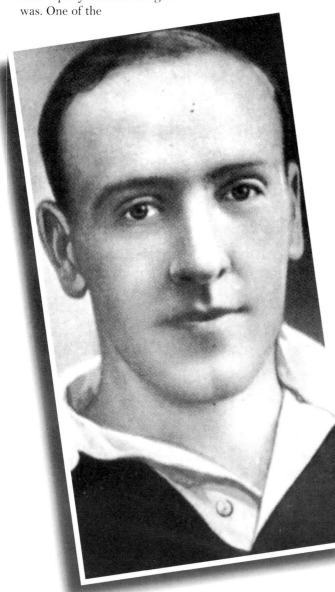

best, and most reliable, full-backs in the business.

First and foremost, he had an uncanny positional sense and, like all such players, he seemed to attract the ball to himself, as steel to a magnet.

Then he was a fine tackler, his timing and strength rarely allowing his opposing winger to come away with the ball.

And finally the length and accuracy of his kicking was superb. Many times he turned defence into attack by landing the ball at the feet of a colleague anything up to 50 yards away. He saw himself as the instigator of attacks.

The wild, hurried and thoughtless clearance was simply not part of his wide repertoire.

He made his first-team debut, aged 18, at the beginning of his second season at Stamford Bridge in September 1926, one of six Scotsmen in the Chelsea line-up that afternoon. Partnering him, at right-back, was a fellow Glaswegian, George Smith, a fine and experienced tutor with some 250 first-team games behind him. A quick and willing learner, Law was, from that day, the undisputed choice for his position for the next decade, absent from his post only when injured.

Twice he represented his country, and both times against England, most notably when the legendary 'Wembley Wizards' won their famous 5-1 victory in 1928. Modestly Law shrugged off his part, "I was little more than a spectator. The ball always belonged to our forwards." Then, adding a postscript which says much for his character, "my only regret was that George Smith wasn't playing. He was a better full-back than I was."

Latterly injury dogged his career, and he was absent for the whole of the 1934–35 campaign. But for that, his number of first-team appearances, 319, would have been considerably higher as, no doubt, would his tally of goals scored, 19, the majority summarily dispatched from the penalty spot.

In the early spring of 1938, having apparently been pensioned off to pass on his knowledge to the reserve and 'A' team recruits, he was recalled to the senior colours for a handful of games, his pace now even more restricted by age and surgery. Still, the style and thoughtful intention were there and he, nostalgically, gave pleasure to many as he took his final bow.

Tommy played for no other professional club, his loyalty to Chelsea showing through when he turned his back on an offer from the French club Nîmes, who had enticed others by hiring their services for £20 a week at a time when the basic maximum wage in England was £8.

Like Wilson, he spent his Saturday afternoons in his declining days at The Bridge well into the 1960s, a fascinating raconteur, and, of course, still part of Chelsea.

The Riddle Remains Unsolved

DAVID Calderhead's successor, in the spring of 1933, was Leslie Knighton whose previous managerial experience included service with Huddersfield Town, Manchester City, Arsenal, Bournemouth and Birmingham. His objective was clear enough. After a quarter of a century of a disappointingly limited measure of success, given the talent available, could he solve the 'Chelsea riddle'? Greatly respected for his fairness in dealing with players, by coming to Stamford Bridge he was facing the greatest challenge of his career.

In theory he had everything a new incumbent could desire; a marvellously gifted squad of players; ambitious directors prepared to support him financially; a stadium capable of accommodating 80,000 spectators; and a loyal army of supporters supplemented by a sizeable retinue of non-partisans, for whom Stamford Bridge was the most convenient ground in London as regards accessibility, attracted by a club with a reputation of providing high entertainment.

Knighton did not wait long to discover the size of the task confronting him. The view that he had the tools to do the job was reinforced when his first Chelsea team took the field with six international players in the line-up, among them Johnny ('Jake') Jackson, Scotland's goalkeeper who was to contest that position at Chelsea with Woodley up to the outbreak of war. Yet, Stoke City won this opening fixture in the Potteries by a single goal.

After seven matches, and two points, Chelsea were once more propping up the table, and faced with a worrying injury crisis. From this start they never recovered. In a scenario all too familiar, they were five points adrift of the rest of the field by Christmas, with Knighton rarely in position to pick his strongest team.

Fortunately, five points from three games over the

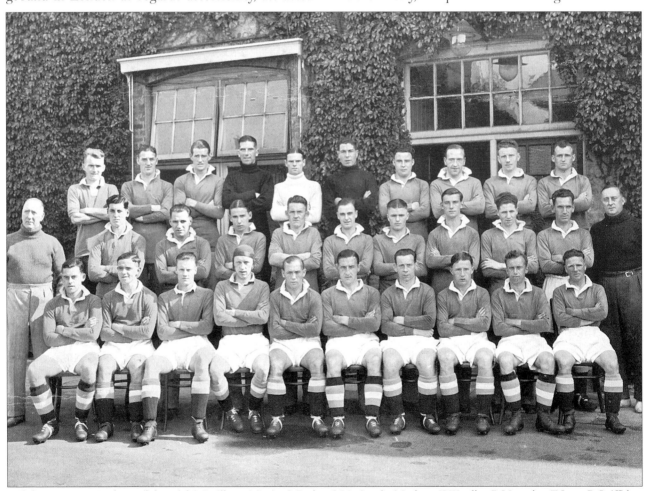

Chelsea, 1933-34. Back row (left to right): L.Allum, A.Craig, G.Barber, S.Macintosh, J.Jackson, V.Woodley, R.Macaulay, T.Law, R.Griffiths, W.Mitchell. Middle row: J.Whitley (trainer), P.O'Dowd, S.Dudley, P.Buchanan, J.O'Hare, W.Pollock, W.Brown, C.Sime, W.Russell, J.Rankin, C.Harris (assistant trainer). Front row: A.Oakton, J.Copeland, W.Chitty, T.Priestley, H.Gallacher, G.Gibson, J.Horton, S.Prout, H.Miller, J.Crawford.

In March 1934, Alex Cheyne, who had been playing for the French club Nimes, along with Andy Wilson, returned to Chelsea. Hughie Gallacher and other members of the Chelsea team welcome him back to Stamford Bridge.

Chelsea, 1935-36. Back row (left to right): Odell, Russell, Law, Allum, Woodley, Barber, Macaulay, Chitty. Middle row: Copeland, O'Hare, Hutcheson, Mitchell, Jackson, Griffiths, Mills, Argue. Front row: Spence, Cheyne, Gibson, Bambrick, Craig, Barrowclough, Burgess, Horton.

holiday period proved a turning point and although Chelsea were again bottom of the list at the end of March, at least the gap was minimal, so that a burst of five consecutive victories enabled safe harbour to be reached, finally thanks to a 2-2 draw with Arsenal, in front of 65,000 anxious supporters. In February another defeat at Stoke had brought Chelsea's FA Cup prospects to an abrupt halt.

Apart from Oakton and Woodley, whose outstanding form kept Jackson in the reserve team after the Scot had recovered from injury, every other recognised first-choice player was absent on at least ten occasions. Mills and Gallacher, sharing the centre-forward berth, scored 27 times between them. Notable newcomers were the Irish terrier wing-half Billy Mitchell from Distillery, Jimmy Argue, from Knighton's former club Birmingham, and a Scottish full-back John O'Hare. All three were to justify their signings in the years ahead.

The most curious happening, in a season in which Chelsea's image remained unchanged, was the selection of Jackson to keep goal for Scotland against England at Wembley in April, after more than six continuous months of Combination football. Not since 13 September had he been chosen for the first team.

Nor did the 1934–35 season change matters. Bottom of the First Division file at the end of September, one Saturday evening newspaper misprinted their only victory, 3–1 against Leicester City, as '33–1'. More good material for the stage comedians whom Chelsea, as usual, delighted considerably more than their long-suffering supporters.

Right, top: Just part of the record crowd of 82,905 who jammed into Stamford Bridge to see the visit of Arsenal in October 1935. It was the biggest attendance ever seen at a Football League game up to that time.

Right, bottom: Chelsea's new signing Irish international defender Cecil Allen (centre) is greeted by Joe Bambrick, a fellow Irish international, after arriving at Stamford Bridge in November 1935. Manager Leslie Knighton looks on.

Gallacher's increasingly tempestuous days in London came to an end when he was transferred to Derby County in October, whereupon the reliable and persevering Mills was, needlessly one would have thought, replaced at centre-forward by the signing of Joe Bambrick, Linfield's Irish international. A more permanent acquisition was Dick Spence. A miner from Barnsley, with eyes that sparkled and feet that twinkled at great speed down either wing, he remained at Chelsea as player and, later, youth-team trainer for nearly 40 years. His record as the oldest 'Pensioner' to play in the League side (40 years 57 days) may well stand for ever.

Although this time finishing in mid-table, the see-saw nature of results continued. Bambrick and Spence brought much-needed punch to the attack, the winger's 19 goals from their combined tally of 34 being a remarkable return after not making his debut until the second half of September. It was another Chelsea all-time best.

The 1935–36 season opened on a note of sadness. Bert Palmer, assistant-secretary since 1907, died, and almost immediately news came of the deaths of

J.T.Mears, a founder director, and chairman Claude Kirby, who had also occupied his post since 1905. But if things on the field were scarcely happier for the first six months, a late flourish, beginning in mid-March, propelled the team into the top half of the table to finish in their highest position for 16 years (eighth).

The crowds continued to flock in, some 82,905 of them on 12 October to see the home fixture with Arsenal. Not only was this a new record for any attendance at Stamford Bridge but it was also the highest number of spectators to be recorded at any English Football League game up to that time.

One reason was undoubtedly the flow of goals. Bambrick, Spence and Mills all reached double figures, as did Harry Burgess. At the age of 31 he was signed from Sheffield Wednesday after a distinguished career which included four English international caps. For four seasons he was to serve Chelsea with distinction, and success.

Woodley, keeping Jackson out of the limelight, was on the verge of his England career, Law still operated at left-back, when fit, and the Mitchell-Craig-Miller trio was the solid backbone of the side. At inside-forward Scotsman George Gibson was a typical

Vic Woodley is beaten as Fulham take the lead in the FA Cup fifth-round replay at Craven Cottage in February 1936. The Cottagers went on to win 3-2.

Sam Weaver, Chelsea's new 'international star' as he was billed, is greeted by Tommy Law after joining Chelsea in August 1936. From left to right are: Barrowclough, Whitley, Law, Bambrick, Weaver, Barber and O'Hare.

Birmingham's Harry Hibbs punches off the head of Chelsea's Dick Spence at Stamford Bridge in September 1936. Chelsea lost 3-1.

Vic Woodley
– Goalkeeper Supreme

FOR the three seasons leading up to 1939-40, when football was disrupted by the outbreak of war, quite simply Victor Robert Woodley was, the best goalkeeper in England. Among his rivals for his international jersey were Frank Swift, at 23, coming to his prime, Charlton Athletic's flamboyant Sam Bartram, Harry Hibbs now aged 30 but still a fine 'keeper, and Bob Hesford at Huddersfield Town. The cupboard was more than well-stocked with candidates for this crucial position.

Yet, it was Woodley who set a new record by being selected to keep goal in 19 consecutive internationals, a run which would undoubtedly have been extended but for the unfortunate interruption of football's peacetime competitions in September 1939.

In 1931 there was a successful play running in the West End entitled 'Young Woodley', as Chelsea's young recruit soon became known. Sam Millington was then approaching the end of his long and distinguished goalkeeping career, and deputy 'keeper Sam McIntosh was untried.

One season in the reserve team was enough to reveal Woodley's undoubted potential, immediately confirmed by a brief introduction to first-team duty early in 1931-32. After initial nervousness, he showed his quality and, on Millington's retirement, 12 months later, he was the obvious replacement. For Chelsea as a whole it was a disappointing season and there were weaknesses in defence for which Woodley's comparative inexperience was not by any means responsible.

Be that as it may, by the time the 1933-34 season came round Chelsea had signed Scotland's reigning international goalkeeper, John Jackson, who immediately ousted his youthful rival. Five matches into the season, however, an unfortunate injury to Jackson let in Woodley once more and, for virtually the rest of the 1930s it was the Englishman who was considered first choice.

Fortunately, the two became firm friends and Jackson showed great restraint and patience by uncomplainingly accepting Combination football, and on three occasions was pitchforked into international matches direct from Chelsea's reserve team.

Woodley had never kept goal until, having left school, he took over the position in an emergency for his local village team. Once he played for Reading Reserves as an amateur, but it was while playing for Windsor and Eton that he was noticed by a Chelsea scout.

In discussions about England's top 'keepers down the years, Woodley's name figures less prominently than it deserves. He was quite outstanding and wonderfully reliable with an uncanny sense of anticipation. In the autumn of his career, with eyesight failing, a playing colleague never ceased to be amazed how forwards always 'fired straight at him'.

In the last five or so years before 1939, it was Woodley's immaculate performances which, more than any other factor, preserved Chelsea's First Division status.

Essential war work kept both him and Johnny Jackson in London throughout the war. Often they shared the goalkeeping duties, and for a period the Scotsman turned out as a guest player for Brentford. By 1944 Jackson had retired and Woodley, for six years deprived of full-time training and now in his mid-30s, was not as sharp or agile as he had been. He kept goal for the Pensioners in the 1944 wartime Wembley Final, and against Dynamo Moscow in November 1945, but a month later he had been put out to grass with Bath City.

But not quite. Early in 1946 the veteran answered a cry for help from Derby County, beset with injuries to both their regular goalkeepers, and four months later he found himself performing at the highest level once more in the first post-war FA Cup Final, won by Derby 4-1.

Even then he was not quite finished and had the audacity to return to Stamford Bridge on Easter Saturday 1947 playing for the Rams, to an emotional welcome – and a sad farewell.

'Young Woodley' had ended, as he had begun, enormously respected as a performer in the highest class of all.

Woodley clears from a Wolves attack at Stamford Bridge in 1937. His fellow defender is George Barber.

Chelsea reinforcement. A marvellous entertainer, on his day his brilliant skills thrilled crowds everywhere. He was even once described as 'Chelsea's Alex James'.

Surprisingly, again, no impact was made in the FA Cup, Second Division Luton had beaten the Blues at the first hurdle in 1935, and this time neighbours Fulham ended the Wembley dream of a team potentially well-equipped to reach the Final.

Nor did Knighton's fourth season at the helm in 1936-37 bring any joy. Sam Weaver, the long-throw expert, converted from inside-forward to wing-half, came as an expensive replacement for the ageing Miller.

Starting with two wins, following a highly successful European summer tour, which included only one defeat in the last fixture of a gruelling and crowded schedule, the domestic programme followed an uneventful course, for once lacking in the excitement of the wrong sort so often experienced in the lowest reaches of the table. In steering clear of trouble, however, only once did Chelsea trespass above the halfway mark. Having striven in vain for consistency for 30 years, perhaps it was not such a good idea after all!

Apart from Weaver, there was no change in personnel. Bambrick, injured for much of the time,

Dick Spence bothers Turner, the Fulham goalkeeper, in a fourth-round FA Cup tie at Stamford Bridge in January 1939. Chelsea won 3-0 on their way to the quarter-finals. Jimmy Argue looks on.

The Chelsea forward line in February 1939. From left to right: Spence, Payne, Mills, Argue, Hanson.

Joe Payne has bad luck, heading just wide of the Aston Villa goal at Stamford Bridge in March 1939.

allowed Mills a more regular claim to the centre-forward spot many felt should have been his, without challenge, for some time. His 22 goals certainly supported this view.

Tommy Law's career had reached its twilight stage and O'Hare joined George Barber in partnership at full-back. Six players occupied the left-wing position without any staking a regular claim. At the other end of the field Jackson, uncomplainingly, was allowed only one outing, taking over from Woodley who made his international debut for England against Scotland at Hampden Park. He might well have been confronted by his club colleague at the other end of the park, and so real was this possibility that a third experienced goalkeeper, Willie Gold, from Wolverhampton Wanderers, was signed to cover such an emergency. In fact, he was never required for first-team duty and remained at Stamford Bridge for one season only.

Liverpool were Chelsea's first visitors in 1937-38 and, in the official programme's 'Chelsea Chatter' column, four paragraphs projected at great length the virtues of the club's 'team of talent'. A Mills hat-trick, in a 6-1 victory against the Anfield team, spoke even louder than the lavish prose of the writer. Two defeats followed, however, without a goal being scored, and it was soon clear that the mixture was likely to be 'as before', although not until a spell of seven wins from nine games brought Chelsea level at the top of the

table in October, bracketed with Brentford who possessed superior goal-average.

The fixture planner had obviously looked into his crystal ball, for the following week the 'Bees' were the visitors at The Bridge. Four players were missing on international duty, and Weaver, the captain, absent through injury, but a crowd of almost 57,000 saw goals from Jimmy Argue and Joe Bambrick send the Blues two points clear at the head of the championship table.

More true to tradition, and the predictions of the cynics, the next 16 games brought a mere single victory and, when the return match with Brentford took place five months later, Chelsea were once more back in the familiar surroundings in the lower half of the division.

To be fair, there was a generous ration of injuries. One or two new names staked their claims, among them centre-half Bob Griffiths, for so long left in the shadows by the consistency of Allan Craig, and a somewhat wayward genius, Peter Buchanan who was promptly called up by the Scottish selectors for his first, and only, international cap.

In March, £5,000 was spent to secure the services of 'Ten-Goal' Joe Payne, from Luton, to ensure the long line of distinguished Chelsea centre-forwards should continue. Less easy to follow was the acquisition of Ned Barkas, who had begun his League career with Huddersfield Town as long ago as 1921.

High spirits on the Chelsea training ground as skipper Sam Weaver is tossed into the air on the eve of the 1939–40 season.

For four games he found himself in partnership with Tommy Law, provoking a retort from one season ticket-holder, "That must be a record; the combined ages of our full-backs is 80!" The man, if not a mathematician, nevertheless, was not too wide of the mark.

By the time Liverpool again provided Chelsea's first opposition, in the new season of 1938-39, this time at Anfield, war clouds were gathering and an air of uncertainty prevailed. Adolf Hanson, from Liverpool, and Welsh full-back Jack Smith, were the only signings of note, but apart from three consecutive victories in the opening weeks, which promised better things, Chelsea spent the entire season in the basement region of the table and, not until the penultimate fixture was their safety guaranteed. Payne, with 17 goals, often in partnership with Mills, proved he could unlock First Division defences, but the team was growing old together and fresh blood and young legs were needed.

At least the 'Old Guard' roused themselves for the challenge of the knock-out competition. First out of the hat in each of the first four rounds was a wonderful stroke of fortune. Arsenal were the first victims, sent on their way by two goals from flame-haired Jimmy Argue after a tremendous tussle. 'Team work did it,' one scribe acclaimed, highlighting a quality not very often to the fore in the 1930s. Next in line were Fulham, three clear goals being a comfortable margin, but one which failed to impress one critic. 'Chelsea scarcely deserved to win', he grumbled.

Sheffield Wednesday were tougher customers and only after a five-hour struggle did goals from Burgess (two) and Joe Payne, in the third game at Highbury, provide a passport into the quarter-final.

Grimsby Town, then a respected First Division club, seemed not to present an insuperable obstacle. But, on a treacherous surface, a goal from the appropriately named Frank Crack was the only score of a depressing afternoon, this coming in a brief interval when Allan Craig was absent from his post, receiving treatment off the field for a cut on his head. The fact that over 330,000 had watched the six Cup games was small consolation, except, maybe, for the bank manager.

Before the season ended it was announced that Leslie Knighton was relinquishing his post as manager and would be succeeded by Billy Birrell, a Scot with a long and distinguished playing career, who already had managerial experience with Queen's Park Rangers.

An era was ending. Eight players, among them Law, Barkas, Miller and Gibson were given free transfers and the outbreak of World War Two was less than four months distant. Of the Chelsea team that turned out for the final fixture in September 1939 only Spence and Argue (one game) played League football for Chelsea again. Woodley enjoyed a brief 'second career' with Derby County, crowned by an FA Cup winners' medal at Wembley in 1946, and Weaver and Payne made a dozen appearances between them, with other clubs, before retiring altogether.

Unwanted Interlude

IN THE autumn of 1939, before the new manager, Billy Birrell, together with his adjutant, South African Arthur Stolley who had succeeded Jack Whitley as head trainer, had time to reveal his hand by getting down to the urgent task of rebuilding a team in dire need of repair, World War Two had started. By this time, three League games had already been played, with two young players, Welshman Dai James and Jackie Smith from Port Vale, appearing in the forward line. Both found their way on to the score-sheet. Neither ever played League football again.

Within seven weeks of war starting, regional competitions had been organised up and down the country with 'guest' players permitted to turn out, without restriction. In an atmosphere totally removed from the 'real thing', Chelsea ploughed an undistinguished furrow until appearing in the Football League South Cup Final at Wembley in April 1944, their first-ever appearance at the Empire Stadium.

Charlton Athletic won the game easily enough, by three goals to one. Chelsea's only score coming from a Joe Payne penalty. Payne apart, the only other Chelsea registered players were Woodley, Dick Foss, who had played a handful of first-team games before the war, and Jimmy Bowie, spotted while playing services football in the Royal Navy.

Twelve months later, in the Final of the same competition, Chelsea beat Millwall 2-0, although it was a somewhat hollow triumph, since English internationals Leslie Smith (Brentford) and Len Goulden (West Ham United) were hastily recruited just for this one game to make their debuts for the Blues.

But that was very much the flavour of wartime football and certainly it provided much-needed entertainment for a steadily increasing number of spectators, as well as undoubtedly raising civilian morale in those dark times.

As might be expected, Chelsea recruited some big names whenever possible, among them, Matt Busby (on three occasions), George Hardwick, later England's right-back and captain, Walter Winterbottom, who was to become the first England manager, Scottish winger Billy Liddell, Tommy Walker, soon to sign for Chelsea on a permanent basis, and Eddie Hapgood, pensioned off by Arsenal.

Going to The Bridge in those days could be an exciting experience. With the 'air-raid spotter' stationed on the roof of the old East Stand, it was anyone's guess who might emerge from the tunnel turning out for friend or foe. And, on at least one occasion, at Watford, an unidentified soldier from the terraces rushed to the dressing-room to pull on a Chelsea shirt.

By August 1945, with VE and VJ Days duly celebrated, serious thought turned towards the post-war construction of football teams up and down the country. 'Guest' players were still permitted in the now restructured regional leagues but, although welcome, it became increasingly recognised as a short-sighted policy which did little for longer-term planning and recruitment.

That season the FA Cup competition was relaunched, of course with only registered players allowed to play for their clubs, as things rapidly returned towards normality.

Chelsea, in the meantime, had not been idle. Already they had signed several of their longer resident guests. Danny Winter (Bolton Wanderers) and John Harris (Wolverhampton Wanderers) were to become defensive stalwarts for several seasons. Goulden had moved across London, from West Ham

Chelsea goalkeeper John Jackson in action against Brentford at Griffin Park in October 1939 during a Football League South Group 'B' match as the wartime competitions got under way. The other Chelsea player is Bob Salmond. Holliday is the Brentford centre-forward.

Above: Charlton goalkeeper Sam Bartram, guesting for Millwall, turns the ball around his post for a corner as Chelsea press in the Football League South Cup Final at Wembley in April 1945.

Below: Chelsea's Ian Black tips the ball over the bar from a Millwall attack at Wembley. The right-back covering the goal is Danny Winter. Black, an Aberdeen player, guested for Chelsea whilst serving in the REME. He later had a good career with Fulham.

Chelsea players, looking rather self-conscious with their bouquets presented by the Dynamo Moscow players before the start of the famous match against the Russian tourists at Stamford Bridge in November 1945. From left to right: Harris, Woodley, Tennant, Bacuzzi, Taylor, Russell, Lawton, Buchanan, Goulden, Williams, Bain.

United. And, most spectacularly of all, Tommy Lawton generally recognised as the outstanding centre-forward in the land at that time, had been obtained from Everton, for a fee of £11,500.

As at other times in their history, Chelsea were 'thinking big' and sparing no money or effort to bring success to Stamford Bridge at last. In addition, other recruits came from services football. Goalkeeper Bill (Harold) Robertson, full-back Freddie Lewis, half-backs Bobby Russell, Alex Machin and Jimmy Macaulay and forwards Jimmy Bain, Len Dolding and Johnny Galloway (a pre-war player from Glasgow Rangers).

From the 1939–40 staff only Dicky Spence, Jimmy Argue, Dick Foss, Albert Tennant, Alex White and Joe Payne remained, only one of whom, the evergreen Spence, resumed with any regularity.

Enormous crowds flocked in once more, 53,000 watching Tommy Lawton's debut, in a 'bread-and-butter' regional league game, three days before Chelsea staged one of the most prestigious fixtures ever played at The Bridge.

In November 1945, Dynamo Moscow Football Club arrived for a four-match tour of Britain and

Chelsea provided the first opposition. It is safe to say that never before had such interest been shown in any match played at the stadium.

Soon after breakfast the crowds started to arrive. Hastily, the gates were opened minutes after midday, only to be shut again an hour before kick-off. How many gained entry into Stamford Bridge that day can never be known. Some 74,496 customers paid for admission, with thousands more swarming into the ground, having invaded the adjoining gardens of properties in Fulham Road and clambering over gates and walls in order to see the match. Hundreds gained a superb, if perilous, viewing point from the roof of the East Stand. Still more watched from the greyhound racing track or lined the touch-lines. Unofficial estimates put the crowd at 100,000.

The Russians had prepared for the tour with special training at a camp in the Caucasus Mountains. Their fitness was superb and clearly contrasted with that of Chelsea's still part-timers. Indeed, the Russians' pre-match warm-up training was itself breathtaking.

Against all probability Chelsea were two goals ahead by half-time, thanks to Goulden and Reg

The Dynamo Moscow team march on to the field clutching the flowers which they gave to their opponents.

mander G.Clark who allowed an obviously 'offside goal' from Dynamo to stand to make the final score 3-3.

What did it matter? No one present will ever forget the game, or the occasion. And Dynamo continued on their merry way, overwhelming Cardiff City (10-1) and beating Arsenal, including 'star-of-the-day' Stanley Matthews (4-3 in thick fog at White Hart Lane), before they rounded off their tour with a draw 2-2 against Glasgow Rangers to conclude a brief, but memorable, chapter in English football.

During this transitional season of 1945-46, the FA Cup was played for the first, and only, time on a two-leg 'home and away' basis. Chelsea eliminated both Leicester City and West Ham United before Aston Villa won both the fifth-round games by a single goal to end any hope of a 'hat-trick' of Wembley appearances in successive seasons. Nearly 300,000 had watched the six games and, most important, of all, 'normal' football had returned after seven seasons of unreality and 'make-do'.

A final, and most pleasant postscript to wartime football was Chelsea's visit to Denmark to play KB Copenhagen as part of that club's 70th anniversary celebra-

Khomich, the Dynamo Moscow goalkeeper, tips over from a Chelsea attack. The massive crowd, estimated at 100,000, is crammed right up to the touch-lines at Stamford Bridge.

Williams, a highly talented recruit from Watford. A Dynamo goal soon after half-time was quickly followed by the equaliser, whereupon Lawton responded with a typically brilliant header and a famous Chelsea victory seemed assured until a controversial (or was it a diplomatic?) decision from referee Lieutenant Com-

tions, at the end of April 1946. A charming greeting from the club chairman welcomed the Blues. "To us in KB the name of Chelsea has always been surrounded by a special halo because of Nils Middelboe's long and happy association with your club. Therefore there is no club we would rather see than Chelsea."

Dick Spence
– Long-staying Sprinter

Peter Bonetti and Ron Harris, apart, no player's span as a first-team player at Chelsea has exceeded that of Dicky Spence.

At first sight, on or off the field, he looked every inch a Cockney. Standing 5ft 7ins and weighing around 9st, he was a buoyant, chirpy little character, invariably smiling and friendly.

So far as his background was concerned nothing was further from the truth; Spence was born and reared in the South Yorkshire, in Barnsley in the heart of one of the country's greatest coal-mining areas.

Early on an ability as a schoolboy footballer set his heart on becoming a professional, earning his living above ground. Centre-forward was his first preference, but such a position was no place for a welterweight in the hurly-burly of the adult game, played by miners on uneven surfaces amongst the pitheads, and so he moved to the less congested areas on the wings.

Dicky was to prove one of Leslie Knighton's best acquisitions, arriving at Stamford Bridge with By the time the curtain fell on that campaign he had scored 19 goals in the remaining 34 fixtures, a record for a Chelsea wingman which has never been exceeded. eight League games of the season's fixtures already gone in the October of 1934.

Speed, and acceleration, were his most lethal weapons. Down either flank (he preferred the right on his stronger foot), he left defenders, often less mobile and heavier built in those days, trailing in his wake giving centre-halves the poser of deciding whether or not to abandon their posts in the middle.

Frequently, he settled the matter himself by scoring a goal, before they had recognised the danger.

Lightness on his feet, and possessing a full bag of tricks, was explained by his small frame. What was less easy to account for was the power of his shooting which constantly found the best goalkeepers of his time utterly taken by surprise and left flat-footed.

Unfortunately, his rise to the top coincided with the Stanley Matthews era. And there were others in the right-wing queue for an England place also. Twice, however, he wore his country's shirt, in 1936 against Austria and Belgium.

During the war, Spence joined the Metropolitan Police Reserve, surely one of the more improbable members of the force? Doubtless his speed in dealing with emergencies was thought to be sufficiently valuable to outweigh other more obvious physical deficiencies. And indeed it was reported on one occasion that he had, single-handed, apprehended a 'blackout car thief! Certainly he would have enjoyed the funny side of that situation, as he did of so many others.

Inon he operated on his familiar beat, aided now by such able lieutenants as Tommy Walker and Len Goulden, and with the additional target of Tommy Lawton's head, always threatening, and converging up on goal.

A broken leg ended his first-team days, but not before he had become the oldest player in Chelsea's history to play League football, one month past his 39th birthday. Another record which may well stand for all time. 1946 it was back to normal with Spence on Chelsea's right wing, the sole survivor of the pre-war team. For one seas

As an essential part of the furniture, Dick remained at The Bridge on the training staff for another two decades or so, usually travelling with the 'A' team or Juniors. His still speedy forays on to the field, with sponge dripping, to attend to injury, evoked memories of earlier times, often raising he biggest cheer of the match.

Popular and recognised to the end, he never left the area of London which made him famous and he could be spotted, unobtrusively and still light on those feet, making his way through the gates to support the team he had served so long and so well, doubtless having called in at his favourite bookmaker's on the way to the game.

Back To Business

ON SATURDAY, 31 August 1946, it was back to serious business once more. "After seven, reach-me-down wartime seasons it is football in full dress... football again in grim earnest," as one writer put it.

Within days Chelsea's somewhat thin playing staff had been notably reinforced by the signing of Tommy Walker, at the age of 31 a short-term investment. For £6,000, however, he was to prove a bargain. Soon after, Harry Medhurst moved across London from West Ham, in part-exchange for Joe Payne. And another welcome recruit was an amateur from Switzerland. Already a full international, Willi Steffen had come to England to learn the language and for four months his towering presence at left-back was a big and unexpected bonus.

Under the 'new' manager starting his first normal season at Stamford Bridge after the seven-year hitch, Billy Birrell's team, in true Chelsea tradition, provided excellent entertainment. The Walker-Lawton-Goulden international inside-forward trio were without doubt the most skilful and experienced in England. They shared 50 goals between them, but, alas, that total was never enough to outweigh defensive shortcomings.

Danny Winter, John Harris, with the later addition of Steffen, when available, and goalkeeper Harry Medhurst, all worked overtime to shore up an otherwise uncertain and inexperienced defence. But apart from the two relegated teams no other rearguard proved so vulnerable and a final place of 15th, achieved without alarms, was about par for the course.

The highlights of an unexceptional campaign were the third round FA Cup meetings with Arsenal, themselves very much in a transitional period of team-building. Draws at Stamford Bridge and Highbury were followed by a memorable 2-0 Blues' victory in the third match at Tottenham, a battle set alight by two magnificent Tommy Lawton goals. An aggregate crowd of 180,000 watched the three ties in a season, which was the longest in the history of the Football League, extended until 14 June due to a combination of appalling wintry conditions which lasted into April, and a ban on mid-week afternoon fixtures.

By the time the 1947-48 season started it was clear that Lawton had become unsettled and, after two uneasy months, he had moved, surprisingly, to Third Division Notts County for a, then, record fee of £20,000, with wing-half Bill Dickson moving in the opposite direction as part of the deal.

Clearly the team was still in need of further strengthening and new faces included Welsh international full-back Billy Hughes, along with his Luton Town colleague centre-forward Hugh Billington, both already past the age of 30, Scottish winger Bobby Campbell and, best of all, Roy Bentley, a Bristolian who had made his name with Newcastle United.

The Lawton affair had a long-term unsettling effect and a thoroughly anonymous season ended with Chelsea in 18th position in the table, having failed to progress beyond the fourth round of the Cup.

Nor was the mixture much different the following year. Finishing five places further up the League ladder, and reaching the fifth round in the knock-out competition, was scarcely the stuff, one would have imagined, to pull in the crowds, Yet, incredibly, over a million spectators poured through the Stamford Bridge turnstiles, the highest recorded number up to that time.

Roy Bentley had now

Chelsea in 1946-47, the first post-war season. Back row (left to right): Alex White, Jimmy Argue, John Galloway, Bill Robertson, Tommy Lawton, Len Goulden, Dick Foss, Albert Tennant. Front row: Alex Machin, Joe Payne, John Harris, Danny Winter, Fred Lewis.

Dick Spence finds himself foiled by the diving Leeds United goalkeeper John Hodgson at Stamford Bridge in September 1946 as Len Goulden looks on. Chelsea won 3-0. A week earlier they had lost 7-4 at Anfield.

moved to centre-forward, adopting an unorthodox roving commission that surprised and unsettled many opposing defences. Often operating down either flank, he puzzled and confused the more static and immobile centre-halves of those days, still very much regarded as defensive pivots.

Tommy Walker played his last game for the Blues, against Portsmouth at Fratton Park on Boxing Day 1949, returning to his first love, Heart of Midlothian, with a view to easing his way into football management. Chelsea have had no more popular, or player better-liked by friend and foe alike.

By now Ken Armstrong had made the right-half position his own. Costing the statutory £10 signing

on fee, he joined Chelsea on demobilisation from the Army. A 'one-club' man, he gave 11 years of loyal and distinguished service before emigrating to New Zealand. One appearance for England, in his country's 7-2 victory over Scotland at Wembley, was scant recognition for his polished and artistic play. Along with Walker, he was renowned for his fine sportsmanship and sense of fair play.

Again, 1949-50 was also, thankfully, at least free of relegation worries. Australian wing-half Frank Mitchell was the only newcomer of any standing in defence and Billy Gray, a small tricky and fast winger from the North-East added penetration to the forward line. This time, Chelsea mounted their

Tommy Walker, making his debut for Chelsea, opens the scoring in the 3-0 win over Leeds in September 1946.

The ball seems to have evaded almost everyone in this fourth-round FA Cup tie against Derby County at Stamford Bridge in January 1947. Players from left to right include Willi Steffen, Raich Carter, Jack Stamps, Angus Morrison and John Harris. The game ended in a 2-2 draw and Chelsea lost the Baseball Ground replay 1-0 despite Derby losing their goalkeeper in the first few minutes.

The 1946-47 season was disrupted by dreadful weather and Chelsea played their final League game as late as 26 May. Here in March 1947, on a snow-bound Stamford Bridge, Blackpool's Stan Mortensen (second from left) scores his side's first goal in their 4-1 victory.

strongest FA Cup challenge for 18 years with some memorable contests along a road which, many would claim undeservedly, ended tantalisingly short of the Wembley Final itself.

Brentford, at Griffin Park, presented little problem in the first chapter, with Jimmy Bowie scoring the only goal of the match. The next round brought Newcastle United down the Fulham Road and, on a frost-bound playing surface, the Geordies were defeated, 3-1, after a game of much skill and high drama, brought to its climax by one of the finest goals ever seen at Stamford Bridge.

With Chelsea a man short through injury, and precariously hanging on to their 2-1 lead, Bentley, uncharacteristically operating in defence, cleared a Newcastle corner-kick, enabling Bobby Campbell to set off on a 50-yard dash over the ice, leaving the only covering defender in his wake *en route*, and slipping the ball into the net past the goalkeeper.

Chesterfield were the next victims, in a replay, a convincing 3-0 win at The Bridge giving the Pensioners a plum home draw against Manchester United in the sixth round.

By 2pm on an early March afternoon, all gates had been closed with more than 70,000 spectators inside the ground and ticket-holders fighting their way through others locked out, yet reluctant to abandon hope and miss what turned out to be one of the finest games seen at the stadium.

Bobby Campbell scored for Chelsea after six minutes and, although clearly the superior team, not until another epic goal well into the second half, this time

from Bentley, was the tension lifted. A clever back-heel from Billy Gray found the centre-forward several yards outside the United penalty area. Receiving the ball on his left, and quickly transferring it on to his right foot, he smashed an unstoppable shot into the top left-hand corner of the net, to put the Blues into a semi-final against old rivals, Arsenal, at White Hart Lane.

By this time many supporters were convinced that, at long last, this was to be 'Chelsea's year'. And after 25 minutes of that semi-final even the doubters were convinced. Two goals from the flamboyant Roy Bentley had surely ensured a passage into the Cup Final. Len Goulden, recalled from semi-retirement, was his old masterly self, constantly opening gaps in the Arsenal defence. Behind him John Harris had his defence, well organised and seldom under pressure.

But, on the stroke of half-time, a freak goal changed everything. Freddie Cox, Arsenal's right winger, took a corner with the outside of his right foot which was aimed at the near post, before it suddenly appeared to swerve past Billy Hughes and then beat Medhurst's late, unavailing, lunge to punch the ball clear.

Never again could Chelsea re-establish their earlier supremacy. The famous Compton brothers, Leslie and Denis, together engineered an equaliser and in the replay four days later, Arsenal more than deserved their one-goal victory, the winner almost inevitably coming from Cox.

No one present on either of those occasions will forget the contrasting emotions first of rising elation, and then of utter despair.

Roy Bentley gets the betters of Arsenal's Archie Macaulay at Highbury in March 1948. Joe Mercer looks on. Bentley and Campbell scored the goals in Chelsea's 2-0 win over the Gunners.

Bentley races in as Birmingham City's Gil Merrick gathers the ball at Stamford Bridge on New Year's Day 1949. Chelsea won 2-0.

Without doubt the two games marked the high point of Birrell's 13 years as manager.

The following season, 1950–51, certainly produced drama, but of a very different sort. As so often in earlier days, First Division survival became the objective. Somehow the depression inflicted by that semi-final defeat never dispersed, its psychological effect persisting. Apart from two new full-backs, Sid Bathgate and Stan Willemse, replacing the Welshmen Winter and Hughes, there were few changes in personnel but, somehow, the vital spark was missing.

By early April all seemed lost. With four fixtures remaining, Chelsea, without a win in 14 games, were marooned at the bottom of the table four points adrift of Sheffield Wednesday (21st) and six behind Everton (20th).

Three of the four final games were at home, with the other match against Fulham at Craven Cottage. At this point Billy Birrell decided to replace Harry Medhurst in goal with Bill (Gibb) Robertson who had spent almost six years serving his apprenticeship in the reserves and 'A' team. Standing over 6ft and with massive hands, he made his debut, betraying no outward

sign of nervousness, against Liverpool who were beaten 1-0.

Next for the unexpected slaughter came Wolverhampton Wanderers who were sent back to

Bentley in action again, this time challenging for the ball with Fulham centre-half Jim Taylor at Craven Cottage in September 1949. A crowd of nearly 46,000 saw a 1-1 draw.

Chelsea defender Bill Hughes robs Stanley Matthews of the ball – probably only temporarily – in the First Division match against Blackpool at Stamford Bridge in February 1951, a season in which Chelsea flirted dangerously with relegation. The referee is Arthur Ellis.

the Midlands pointless under somewhat unusual circumstances. Chelsea won 2-1, thanks to a Bentley spot-kick awarded after 18-year-old Bobby Smith had toppled over in the penalty area, yards away from his nearest opponent. Heartened by what seemed an idiosyncratic decision on the part of the referee, Ken Armstrong then proceeded to embark on a long dribble, conspicuously controlling the ball with his hand along the route and, with Wolves' defenders relaxing in anticipation of the referee's whistle, put the ball into the net for a goal which, amazingly, was allowed to stand.

Now speculation and excitement were mounting, and a third win, also by a 2-1 margin, against Fulham seemed almost inevitable, to set up a dramatic final day of the season.

By this time Chelsea had at long last moved out of bottom place, ahead of Sheffield Wednesday, on goal average, but still found themselves two points adrift of Everton. Not only that, but the fixture-planner had paired Wednesday and Everton to meet at Hillsborough. A draw would be enough to save the Merseyside team while a Sheffield victory would suffice for the Tykes' provided Chelsea lost at home to Bolton

Tommy Walker OBE
– Chelsea's Ace of Hearts

to be placed on the spot three times before he could take the kick. With steady nerve but hurrying, lest the same misfortune should occur yet again, he nonchalantly flashed his shot past goalkeeper Ted Sagar before he could move.

The youngest of a family of ten, Walker learned the game, like so many of his generation, in the streets and on the green of his native village, Livingstone Station. His ability and great talent were inborn and required little in the way of coaching to express themselves.

Enticing him back to Stamford Bridge in September 1946, at the age of 31, was one of Billy Birrell's most successful coups. Completing an all-star inside trio with Tommy Lawton and Len Goulden, together they gave rich entertainment wherever Chelsea played.

Walker's ball-control was marvellous to behold. His mazy dribbles left defenders trailing in his wake. His acceleration frequently took him clear of opposing defences. As a passer of the ball, his hallmark was the long crossfield ball to the far wing. And he capped it all with his accurate shooting, 24 goals from just over 100 games for Chelsea.

On the field he made a lasting impression. Equally in his spare time he won many admirers. At one time a candidate for the ministry, he was closely involved with church work in South London, and, in particular, with the Camberwell Boys' Club, formed by the Revd. James Butterworth, himself a firm Chelsea supporter. Invitations to assist charities were never turned aside.

All too soon, however, he had gone, unable to resist an invitation to return to his beloved Hearts in January 1949, as player-assistant manager. His final game for Chelsea took place at Fratton Park on Boxing Day. As both teams stood back applauding as he left an English ground for the last time, Field Marshall Viscount Montgomery of Alamein, president of Portsmouth FC, rigidly standing to attention, saluted Tommy as he disappeared from view.

Back in his native land, the 'Ace of Hearts' graduated to manager in 1951, won major trophies for the Edinburgh club, including two League championships. Later he became a director of the club and was awarded the OBE for 'Services to football'.

Tommy died in an Edinburgh hospice on 11 January 1993. A close friend saw him a few days before the end. In his obituary he wrote, 'Despite being obviously ill, he stopped to help a woman, 20 years his junior, off a bus.' To the last he remained what he had always been, the perfect gentleman, on and off the field.

SERGEANT Tommy Walker played half a dozen games as a guest player for Chelsea at the beginning of the 1944-45 season before disappearing overseas to serve King and Country in the Royal Corps of Signals. In that short time his impact was immediate, one supporter being moved to write in and express, "Tommy is the finest type of sportsman and gentleman that ever donned a football jersey; it has given me joy to watch him."

Tommy joined Heart of Midlothian in 1932, winning the first of his 21 international caps three years later. He is perhaps best remembered for the goal from the penalty spot which earned Scotland a 1-1 draw at Wembley in March 1936. So strong was the wind that day, the ball had

Jim Hartnett, the Middlesbrough winger, leaps above Syd Bathgate, the Chelsea full-back, at Ayresome Park in October 1951, when a 30,000 saw a goalless draw.

Wanderers. And if that did not supply enough intrigue yet another ingredient was added as a result of the Hillsborough fixture starting 15 minutes before the game at The Bridge.

In the event, Chelsea won by four clear goals without undue difficulty. Rather, attention soon became focused on the letter 'A' on the old half-time scoreboard at the north-west corner of the ground which was charting the progress of the game up in Sheffield. A half-time score of 3-0 to Wednesday virtually eliminated Everton from the equation but when the figure '6' appeared on the board it became a matter of goal-average, and for the statisticians to determine whether Chelsea's foursome would now be sufficient to ensure safety.

By the time the final whistle was blown the news had spread round the stadium that all was well. Chelsea had survived. by .044 (or 1/25th) of a goal.

Twelve months later Billy Birrell announced his retirement. His final season brought another Cup semi-final, once more against Arsenal at White Hart Lane which, with history repeating itself, was only concluded after a replay on the same ground. This time the Gunners won with a good deal to spare, 3-0, and missing the excitements of the previous occasion. Again, too, Chelsea avoided relegation after a long struggle, this time without the mathematicians being called into action.

Of all Chelsea's 18 managers, none has been more courteous, or kindly, than Mr Birrell. Or indeed more unfortunate. For his first seven years his work was almost entirely confined to administrative matters as the battles of war were being resolved around the globe. Without doubt this took its toll, and the task of keeping the club in the First Division in the difficult immediate post-war years taxed both his health and energy.

Importantly, he left behind a priceless legacy. On 7 February 1948, under the name 'Tudor Rose', a Chelsea Juniors XI played their first match at Stamford Bridge. As the programme notes said, "It will be an occasion of pride and importance …may today be the first of many occasions which the future will hold when a number who first joined the Chelsea Youth Scheme enter our famous arena, as members of the Chelsea first eleven."

Soon Billy Birrell's brain child, sustained by an efficient scouting network, was the envy of clubs up and down the country, as its conveyor belt supplied an unending supply of talent. His shrewdness and foresight have been instrumental in bearing fruit ever since.

Roy Bentley is tackled by Charlton Athletic's Cyril Hammond at The Valley in April 1952. The game ended goalless and Chelsea again ended the season in a lowly position.

Enter Ted Drake – And The Championship At Last

TO SUCCEED Billy Birrell, the board of directors appointed Ted Drake, the famous pre-war Arsenal and England centre-forward of the 1930s who, for the previous five seasons, had been acquiring a growing reputation as manager of Reading. As a player he had been renowned for his aggression, as well as skill, and he certainly lost no time in making his presence felt in his new surroundings.

Addressing Chelsea's long-suffering supporters, he complimented them on their reputation as 'football's fairest crowd', but called for more partisanship. "Too many people come to Stamford Bridge to see a football match," he complained, "instead of cheering Chelsea.

And for years now the players must have been thoroughly sick of all the music-hall publicity. Let's have more people eating, sleeping, drinking Chelsea."

The Chelsea Pensioner was banished from the official badge, the very name never to be uttered again within the precincts of Stamford Bridge.

The 'honeymoon' period lasted for three weeks, ending with a grand four-day climax during which eight goals crashed into the Blackpool and Aston Villa nets, without reply. Spectators, brought up on a diet of unfulfilled promises and perpetual disappointment could not believe their eyes.

It was, of course, too good to last, and when Manchester City arrived for the final fixture of that 1952-53 season, nothing less than a Chelsea win would guarantee avoiding relegation – as had been the case two seasons earlier. Happily, the team, inspired by Drake's rhetoric and goading, once more rose to the occasion, with a 3-1 victory.

By now Bill Dickson had won international recognition for Northern Ireland and was established in the left-half position. Eric Parsons, after a disappointing beginning, was justifying his transfer fee with some scintillating displays on the right wing. And Drake's knowledge of the lower divisions proved invaluable in unearthing talent at bargain prices.

John McNichol (Brighton & Hove Albion), Les Stubbs (Southend United), Frank Blunstone (Crewe Alexandra), Stan Wicks (Reading), Peter Sillett (Southampton) and Ron Greenwood (Brentford) were to prove wonderful investments. In some cases character and reliability compensated for any lack of outstanding ability.

Ted Drake, the new manager of Chelsea, pictured at his desk shortly after taking over at Stamford Bridge in August 1952.

Charlton goalkeeper Sam Bartram fists the ball away from Roy Bentley at Stamford Bridge in February 1953. Over 53,000 spectators saw Chelsea lose 1-0.

In Greenwood's case it was a matter of 'welcome home'. He had first arrived at Stamford Bridge as a young lad in 1940 and, with John Harris established in his centre-half position, had been allowed to drift away after the war ended. Now, seven seasons later, he took over from Harris, who proceeded to extend his long career by moving to right-back.

At least Chelsea made their mark, once again, in the Cup. A four-match marathon against West Bromwich Albion ended successfully, but a three-day interval proved insufficient time to recharge flattened batteries for the next tie, and Birmingham City won a fifth-round meeting at Stamford Bridge by four clear goals, turning to good account what many considered a grossly unfair advantage.

Another of Drake's reservoirs of talent was amateur football. From Walthamstow Avenue came wing-half Derek Saunders and a versatile attacking goalscorer, Jim Lewis. Seamus O'Connell (Bishop Auckland) and Miles Spector (Hendon) were others recruited in this way.

The manager had now had time to diagnose Chelsea's problems and prescribe his remedy. Jack Oxberry (from Reading) took over as head trainer from Norman Smith,

Chelsea players at London Airport in April, ready to fly to Luxembourg where they were to meet the Brazilian club, Olario. Back row (left to right): Bentley, Willemse. Front row: Harris, Robertson, Oxberry (trainer), Blunstone, Armstrong, Stubbs, Wicks, McNichol, Greenwood, Saunders, Parsons, Tennant.

Roy Bentley is in the thick of the action again, this time getting above Sunderland left-half George Aitken at Stamford Bridge in October 1953. The other Sunderland player is Arthur Hudgell. Nearly 57,000 fans saw a 2-2 draw.

and Harry Medhurst was appointed as his assistant. Even so, came a warning: "Our strength may not yet be sufficient for us to expect the winning of major honours, but we have the ability to do a lot better than last season." It was a promise which was kept.

Strangely, the turning point came in a match at West Bromwich towards the end of October. Albion, then on top of the First Division table, won 5-2, but Drake drew great encouragement from Chelsea's defeat. "If we continue to play this type of football our turn will come," was his prediction. And so accurate was this prophecy that the next 22 games brought 13 wins and eight draws. A final place of eighth would have been even better but for three defeats in the closing 'run-in'.

The 1954-55 season, the 50th year of Chelsea Football Club, began with a feeling of high optimism and Drake declaring, "We have broken the back of our task in creating a 'new Chelsea'."

By the end of October, however, it had all again started to go wrong. Five consecutive defeats included a 6-5 reverse at the hands of Manchester United in one of the most memorable games ever seen at The Bridge, in which the 'unknown' Seamus O'Connell marked his Chelsea debut with a hat-trick. A fairy tale which surely no editor of a fiction magazine would accept?

But, starting with a 3-3 draw at Sunderland, the fight back began, with the manager again assuring everyone, "We have broken the barrier." And, indeed, by Christmas

John Harris
– Honest John

WHEN John Harris arrived in London on essential war work in the summer of 1943, it was a marvellous stroke of good fortune for Chelsea Football Club.

John, a Scotsman born in Glasgow, had started his professional career with Swindon Town, before moving to Swansea Town, and Tottenham Hotspur, briefly, and then signing for Wolverhampton Wanderers, shortly before the outbreak of war, to perform the thankless task of understudying Stanley Cullis, England's centre-half and the outstanding player in his position.

Harris came from a good soccer background. His father, Neil, played for Swansea, Newcastle United and Spurs and also managed the South Wales club. In fact, he played one game for Scotland, against England in 1924, before losing his place to Hughie Gallacher.

'Honest John', as one writer described him, was a born leader and captained Chelsea from his first game in a blue shirt, on 28 August 1943, until handing over the responsibility to Roy Bentley more than ten years later.

Two seasons running, in 1944 and 1945, he became Chelsea's first captain to climb the 39 steps up to Wembley's Royal Box to receive wartime Cup Final medals. On the first occasion, from General Eisenhower, it was a losers' memento; on the second he carried away the Cup itself together with his winners' medal, proudly receiving them from the Prime Minister, Mr Winston Churchill.

The same year, he also played his only game for Scotland, an unofficial international, and it was a source of disappointment to him, and his many admirers, that he never won full recognition after the war ended.

Harris dominated the centre of the Chelsea defence, organising those around him with authority and calm competence. He was the ideal tutor for a young player,

ever ready with friendly advice. Consistency was another of his hallmarks. Rarely, if ever, did his performance on the field fall below the standard he himself had set.

Two inches short of six feet, unfortunately he lacked the extra height to exercise the aerial domination of some of his peers. Having said that, he was a fine header of the ball, often climbing above those opponents with a height advantage. Some too, queried his speed. Maybe, there have been faster central defenders, but, if so, John more than compensated for this with an uncanny positional sense. Always, he appeared in the right place at the right time.

When Ted Drake came to manage Chelsea in 1952, Harris, already past his 35th birthday and cleverly disguising the fact, was entering the autumn of his long career. Soon Stan Wicks had arrived as his successor and an era was ending, or so it seemed.

However, young full-back, Peter Sillett was injured in the second match of the 1954-55 championship season and, in an emergency, Drake turned to the old warrior. "I'll play anywhere you say if you feel that I can be of help to the side." came the reply. An answer which was to add a further 30 appearances to his total, already over 300, and ensured the League championship medal which he treasured more than any other reward he received in his long career.

The greeting from the Chelsea crowd on the day the title was won reflected the admiration and warmth with which he was regarded. But soon he had gone. First to Chester, as player-manager, and later to the city of Sheffield, where he served United and later Wednesday, for some 30 years in various capacities with all the dedication and loyalty which were so typical of this fine man.

Newcastle United goalkeeper Ronnie Simpson makes an acrobatic save from Roy Bentley at St James' Park in September 1954, but Chelsea went on to win 3-1 with Bentley scoring twice. When the Magpies came to Stamford Bridge later in the season, Bentley hit them with a hat-trick. The outside-left is Jim Lewis.

Roy Bentley hammers in a shot against Manchester City at Stamford Bridge in January 1955. Dave Ewing is the City defender. Chelsea lost 2-0 and their championship hopes took a severe knock.

Ninian Park, which at length put Chelsea at the top of the First Division for only the third time in their history. But before Fleet Street could digest the fact, and give it the prominence it surely deserved, the London newspaper industry was paralysed by a strike, which continued for some three weeks.

As so often, the season reached its climax at Easter, with four consecutive wins opening up a four-point lead at the top of the table, and nearest rivals, Wolverhampton Wanderers, arriving for their League fixture at The Bridge on 9 April.

Day, Chelsea found themselves only two points adrift of Wolves, who headed the table. Eleven points from a possible 12 was championship form and included a 4-3 victory at Wolverhampton, with Chelsea scoring twice in 60 seconds in the closing minutes of a game in which three seemingly good Chelsea 'goals' were disallowed by an unsympathetic referee.

Ted Drake's drive and aggression had well and truly permeated the dressing-room and, apart from an almost barren period over Christmas, the momentum never lessened with a fifth-round Cup defeat at the hands of Notts County, in retrospect, proving no great disaster.

It was a victory over Cardiff City on 23 March, at

Not since 'Dynamo Day' had the Fulham Road seen such scenes of excitement. Some 75,000 had squirmed their way through the turnstiles before the gates were closed soon after 2pm, with hordes again spilling over on to the greyhound track. Outside, too, disappointed thousands were helplessly milling around, and missing a memorable battle.

On this gloriously sunny afternoon in early spring, Chelsea at once took the initiative and only fine goalkeeping from England's Bert Williams kept the Chelsea forwards at bay. Wolves' attacking power was

Chelsea skipper Roy Bentley, followed by Frank Blunstone and Charlie Thomson, leads out his team in February 1955, as the Pensioners' championship drive gathered pace. Soon the old music-hall joke of Chelsea' footballing 'pensioners' would be consigned to history.

reduced when their centre-forward wrenched a knee in the first half, Roy Swinbourne pluckily staying on until the end despite his mobility being severely handicapped. Bentley nearly scored with a flying header early on; Peter Sillett with an explosive 35-yard drive went agonisingly close; Bentley, again, and O'Connell, missed good

chances from close range, until a quarter of an hour from time, the destiny of both the game, and the championship, was decided.

O'Connell's drive accurately directed towards the top right-hand corner of the goal completely beat Williams, when centre-half Billy Wright, covering his goalkeeper on the line, and with left-hand extended, pushed the ball away to safety.

To the horror of the Chelsea team, to say nothing of the vast crowd, the referee promptly signalled for a corner-kick to be taken. At once surrounded by a sea of protesting blue shirts, the official was unceremoniously jostled towards his linesman for a lengthy consultation before, to the relief of the great majority, he turned and pointed decisively to the penalty spot.

At that time, full-back Peter

Left: Chelsea took time off from their championship campaign to travel to Bristol Rovers for a fourth-round FA Cup tie in January 1955. Here, Roy Bentley shakes hands with the engine-driver at Paddington Station before the train journey to the West Country.

Eric Parsons is beaten to the ball by Sunderland goalkeeper Fraser at Stamford Bridge in March 1955. Chelsea won 2-1.

Bentley heads one of his hat-trick goals in Chelsea's 4–3 win over Newcastle at Stamford Bridge in February 1955. The Magpies' goalkeeper is Ronnie Simpson, who 12 years later won a European Cup winners' medal with Celtic.

Wolves goalkeeper Bert Williams dives at the feet of Johnny McNichol at Stamford Bridge in April 1955. It was the match which effectively decided the championship in Chelsea's favour, ending Wolves' challenge.

Sillett was probably the hardest, and most lethal, kicker of a dead ball in the game, almost all of his 34 goals for the club coming from such situations. As an uncanny silence engulfed the entire stadium, and from a three-pace run up, he connected with his right foot to power the ball underneath Williams' dive and into the bottom left-hand corner of the net. Whereupon a great roar broke the tension, with Sillett disappearing from view, buried beneath his delighted colleagues.

By no means were Wolves finished. They promptly

Peter Sillett scores the vital goal from the penalty spot against Wolves at Stamford Bridge on 9 April 1955.

Eric Parsons watches his header beat Sheffield Wednesday goalkeeper Dave McIntosh at Stamford Bridge in April 1955. Chelsea won 3-0 and the points confirmed them as Football League champions.

rearranged their forward line and twice Johnny Hancock, the smallest man on the pitch, went close to salvaging a late point. First an effort rebounded off a post; then he was obstructed in the penalty area and, having been set up for another shot, saw his drive narrowly miss the far post. Gamely, and with a measure of good fortune, Chelsea held out before, as the final whistle sounded, the entire playing area became transformed into a sea of celebrating spectators of every age, joyously revelling in Chelsea's most famous ever victory in this, their Golden Jubilee season.

Mathematically, the championship was still undecided, but, a fortnight later probability became certainty as Chelsea comfortably beat Sheffield Wednesday, already doomed to relegation, by three clear goals, the

aggregate home attendances at League matches alone passing the one million mark for the first, and only, time.

More memorable on this occasion were the post-match scenes, with the players parading at the front of the directors' box for the speeches to follow.

First, chairman Joe Mears, nephew of founder Gus, came to the microphone to introduce Ted Drake, skipper Roy Bentley and then, emerging from the shadows, John Harris, captain on the field for a decade in war and peacetime, but now missing out on the action on the field 'on the happiest day of my life'. Many a tear was shed unashamedly although the proceedings ended on a note of humour with the crowd repeatedly chanting "We want the rabbit". But Eric Parsons, hero of so many occasions

Chelsea manager Ted Drake congratulates skipper Roy Bentley after the victory over Sheffield Wednesday which sealed the first Football League championship in Chelsea's 50-year history.

in the championship season, for once could not respond. Amidst gusts of laughter and failing to conceal his embarrassment, he remained totally speechless, the only person in that great throng struck dumb.

Two days earlier, the newspaper strike had ended and Fleet Street was therefore able to add its acclaim to an event which so many thought could never happen. And just to complete the Jubilee celebrations, the Chelsea reserves, 'A' team and juniors all won their respective championships to put the icing on the cake.

Heroes all, the Football League championship medal winners were: goalkeepers – Bill Robertson, Charlie Thomson; Full-backs John Harris, Peter Sillett, Stan Willemse; half-backs Ken Armstrong, Stan Wicks, Ron Greenwood, Derek Saunders; and forwards Eric Parsons; John McNichol, Roy Bentley, Leslie Stubbs, Seamus O'Connell, Frank Blunstone and Jim Lewis. Their names are worthily embedded in every Chelsea Football Club history book.

Chelsea, Football League champions 1954–55. Back row (left to right): Stan Willemse, Peter Sillett, Stan Wicks, Charlie Thomson, Bill Robertson, Derek Saunders, Ron Greenwood, Les Stubbs. Front row: Jack Oxberry (chairman), Jim Lewis, Johnny McNichol, Roy Bentley, John Harris, Ken Armstrong, Seamus O'Connell, Ted Drake (manager). On ground: Eric Parsons, Frank Blunstone.

Roy Bentley
— Roy The Rover

FOR almost nine years Roy Bentley was an integral part of the Chelsea scene. Arriving in January 1948, less than three months after the somewhat acrimonious departure of Tommy Lawton, he was probably the most successful of manager Bill Birrell's captures.

Born and bred in Bristol, Roy had played for both the Rovers and City clubs before moving to Newcastle United and becoming a member of one of the most talented forward lines in the country at that time. At £11,000 he was a bargain buy.

His start at Chelsea, however, was not promising. Adapting to a totally different style of play posed its problems. A spell of reserve-team football did not help and his health started to suffer. "I almost felt like packing up" he confessed later. But by the start of the 1949-50 season the situation had changed and Roy had become well integrated into the club and had settled into his new surroundings.

Most crucial of all, Birrell converted him to the centre-forward position. Until then Bentley had been regarded purely as an inside-right, a creator rather than a taker of chances. But he made the transition so easily that it seemed strange that this had not happened earlier.

He was a brilliant header of the ball, outjumping defenders considerably taller than his 5ft 10ins, and, like his predecessor Lawton, appearing to hover in the air like some predatory hawk, which enabled him to direct the ball downward. His speed was deceptive, his shooting powerful and accurate from either foot.

Initially he was given a roving commission by Birrell as leader of the forward line, a tactic which unsettled, and unhinged, opponents unused to such unorthodox methods and opportunism. Later he returned to a more conventional role. But it made little difference. In whatever style, for a time he was simply the most effective centre-forward in England.

First capped by his country against Sweden in 1948-49, his most famous goal in international football was against Scotland in the 1-0 victory which gave England the domestic championship in 1950, and a passport to the World Cup in South America. In all, he scored nine goals from his 12 appearances, a ratio not often exceeded at this level.

The triumph of his Chelsea days, of course, was leading the club to the Football League championship in 1954-55. Later he recalled his sentiments on the famous afternoon in April when the 3-0 victory over Sheffield Wednesday clinched the title. "I could have wept," he said. "I was so happy to hear those Chelsea cheers. That wonderful crowd. They had been taking it on the chin for 50 years and always came up smiling. How well they deserved to have something to cheer about then."

In those days part of the match day scene at The Bridge was seeing Roy casually strolling though the gates before a match with his wife, Vi, and daughter Lorraine, all part of the Chelsea family atmosphere created by Ted Drake.

The championship was the high-water mark and, after just one more season, the tide of success receded as the manager sensibly decided that the time to build a new team had arrived. At 32, Bentley did not form part of his plans. However, Chelsea's loss turned to Fulham's gain, as the Craven Cottage club adapted Roy's talents into becoming a highly successful centre-half. For four seasons he repaid his £8,500 fee with handsome interest, chalking up another 160 senior games, including an FA Cup semi-final appearance and helping the 'Lillywhites', to promotion into Division One in 1959.

Even then, there was a brief postscript with Queen's Park Rangers before, in 1963, he moved into the managerial seat at Reading. Later, he also managed Swansea before working as secretary at both Reading and Aldershot.

Too Briefly – Jimmy Greaves

IN HIS three years in charge of Chelsea, Ted Drake had worked a minor miracle by putting the biggest prize of all in English domestic football into the Stamford Bridge boardroom cabinet. At long last, a rosy future seemed assured for the club.

Events, sadly, were to prove otherwise and Drake's remaining seven seasons brought a return to days of frustration and disappointment. In retrospect, the odds were against him. Seven of the championship team were already past their 30th birthdays, and only Stan Wicks, Peter Sillett and Frank Blunstone were in the early stages of their footballing careers. Furthermore, within 14 months of the start of the 1955-56 season, a serious knee injury ended Wicks' career at a time when he was freely acknowledged to be one of the finest centre-halves in the game, while Blunstone, already by then capped by England, had his career severely disrupted by breaking a leg twice in three seasons. And, for different reasons, little more was seen of the amateurs, Seamus O'Connell and Jim Lewis.

Rebuilding the team in these conditions was always going to be a major task. The Chelsea Youth Scheme was producing an unending stream of talent. Peter Brabrook had already made his debut in the championship side, a raw and somewhat rough-edged Bobby Smith was left on the sidelines, but only by Roy Bentley's consistency.

And others coming on to the scene included Alan Dicks, Ron Tindall, John Compton, Les Allen, Tony Nicholas and Michael Harrison.

Unfortunately for too many of them, they were introduced at a time when a losing team was living on its memories, in some cases further ambition blunted by recent achievement. Mistakenly, gaps were not filled by a leavening of outstanding, established, players. Only three times in these years did Drake lay out large sums of money for the type of player required.

In December 1956, £20,000, then a record fee for a goalkeeper, brought England international Reg Matthews to The Bridge; £10,000 was paid for Manchester United's rugged half-back Stan Crowther, who had joined the Old Trafford club from Aston Villa in the aftermath of the Munich tragedy; and three and a half years later, Chelsea spent £12,500 for the Scottish half-back Bobby Evans, then 32 and some way past his peak.

Otherwise, a succession of teenagers swam, or sank, in unfamiliar waters without having the benefit of experienced instructors around them to help and advise. Brave policy, it may have been, but it did little more than ensure Chelsea's First Division status was maintained without serious hazard.

Following the 1954-55 season, positions of 16th, 13th, 11th, 14th, 18th and 12th adequately tells the story

'Drake's Ducklings'. In August 1956, Ted Drake fielded what was thought to be the youngest line-up in Chelsea's history with Frank Blunstone, at 21, the oldest player in the team to meet Leeds United. They earned a goalless draw. Here, Drake chats with (from left o right) Les Allen (18), Peter Brabrook (18), Ron Tindall (20), Tony Nicholas (18) and Blunstone before the side left for Elland Road.

Arsenal goalkeeper Jack Kelsey grabs the ball from Chelsea's Ron Tindall at Highbury in March 1958. The number-ten is Jimmy Greaves.

of one of the greyest periods in the club's history up to that time. Only once in those years was even the fifth round of the FA Cup reached, and Darlington and Crewe Alexandra were numbered among Chelsea's conquerors as attendances plummeted to their lowest level since the 1920s.

One opportunity to take Chelsea onward into uncharted territory had been spurned in the summer of 1955 when, admittedly on the advice of the Football Association, the club turned down their right of entry to become England's first representatives in the European Cup. In retrospect, it was an extraordinarily ill-timed and unimaginative decision, and one which Manchester United swiftly refused to follow 12 months later.

There was, however, one beacon light which shone through Ted Drake's final years. In August 1957, a slightly-built 17-year-old, from East Ham, burst on to the soccer scene. Jimmy Greaves, whose feats as a goal-scorer, in junior and reserve-team football were already well-known, made his League debut against Tottenham Hotspur at White Hart Lane on the opening day of the season, scoring an equalising goal shortly before the end of a match in which he had constantly caught the eye, weaving his way effortlessly through a bewildered Spurs defence time and again.

That was just the beginning. Three more goals in the two home games which followed confirmed that his was

no ordinary talent and, after a six-week sabbatical in November and December, when his manager sensibly considered he needed this breather, he was produced again on the morning of Christmas Day to put four goals past a mesmerised Portsmouth defence. His 22 goals from 35 League games was to prove his lowest output in his four seasons at Stamford Bridge.

For a time during this winter it seemed as if another successful side might emerge. Peter Sillett and Saunders survived from the championship winners. Matthews had days of brilliance in goal, and John Mortimore, an amateur from Woking, proved an able and dominant successor to Wicks at centre-half. Brabrook won his first English international cap as a fast and tricky right winger and Ron Tindall lead the line with all the panache of youth, scoring 16 goals. With Blunstone an absentee throughout the season, the team was probably only two players short of again being in a position to challenge for honours. The cheque book, however, was never produced and a side, usually containing as many as nine former Chelsea juniors, remained agonisingly just out of reach of the top clubs, despite having done wonderfully well.

At the beginning of April 1960, with Chelsea flirting on the edge of the relegation zone, another gem appeared from the club's junior ranks. Peter Bonetti an 18-year-old goalkeeper, made the step up into top-class football, as naturally as Greaves had done almost two years before. So well did he make the transition that he held his place until the final fixture, despite the return to fitness of both Matthews and Bill Robertson. A month later, he was a member of the first Chelsea team to win the FA Youth Cup. The Final, against Preston North End, was clinched with a 4-1 victory at Deepdale after a 1-1 first-leg draw at Stamford Bridge. Among the names on the team-sheet for those games, apart from Bonetti, were Allan Harris, Terry Venables, Bert Murray and Bobby Tambling, who scored a hat-trick.

Tambling, along with Barry Bridges, had already made an impressive first-team debut in February 1959, both scoring in a 3-2 victory against West Ham United, before being put back into storage to mature before claiming regular places in the 1961-62 season.

Unhappily, by then Jimmy Greaves had departed in controversial, and highly emotional, circumstances when he became one of the first British players to move into European football, by signing for AC Milan in June 1961 at a fee of £80,000 to earn a £15,000 signing-on fee no football club in this country could match, and despite an 11th-hour bid by chairman Joe Mears offering tempting financial inducement to stay at Stamford Bridge as at last

the maximum, wage restriction in England was lifted.

Few present on the occasion will forget Jimmy's last match for the club when he scored all Chelsea's goals in 4-3 win against Nottingham Forest before disappearing down the players' tunnel after being carried off shoulder-high by his army of adoring fans with many a tear being shed.

Jimmy Greaves tries a shot before Leicester's Tony Knapp can block it at Stamford Bridge in October 1958. Greaves did not get on the scoresheet but Chelsea still managed five goals.

Jimmy Greaves watches his shot drop into the far corner of Gil Merrick's goal when Birmingham visited The Bridge in December 1958. It was the only goal of the match.

Five months later Ted Drake had left Chelsea, too. It was the team occupying last place in the table at the end of September 1961 which sealed his fate and he was at once replaced by his chief coach, Tommy Docherty, who had joined the club weeks earlier. It was a sad, but inevitable, parting after the most successful manager in the club's history up to that time had failed to arrest the slide in the team's fortunes.

Years after, Jimmy Greaves nostalgically wrote: "We had more potential than any other team I have ever played for. But you need experienced players to help draw out the potential and we were just a bunch of kids playing it off the cuff and often coming off second best. It was like being at Butlin's, a real holiday camp atmosphere …we were still kids waiting to grow up."

Bottom left: Peter Bonetti, in only his second game for Chelsea, and Arsenal's Billy McCullough have both missed the ball at Highbury in April 1960. A 40,000 crowd saw Chelsea hammer the Gunners 4-1. Below: Jimmy Greaves, who scored a hat-trick in the match, watches as Wolves' Geoff Sidebottom dives across at Stamford Bridge in August 1960. A 41,000 crowd saw a 3-3 draw. Bottom right: Peter Bonetti dives full stretch to punch clear from West Ham United's John Dick at Upton Park in September 1961. At the end of the season Chelsea were relegated.

Everton's Bobby Collins needed three attempts to beat Reg Matthews from the penalty spot at Stamford Bridge in October 1960. The referee ordered the first kick to be retaken, then Matthews blocked the shot with a brilliant save but the ball rebounded to Collins who finally put it in the net.

Jimmy Greaves
Goals – and More Goals

Few players in the entire history of the game have equalled Jimmy Greaves' output of goals. He was at Chelsea as boy and man, for six seasons. After a somewhat modest (on his own standards) 14 goals from 17 South-East Counties League games announced his arrival in 1955-6, he went on, in his first full season as a junior, to clock up 114 goals in all matches the following year. An extraordinary achievement, and one often omitted from the record books, but a feat for which he was presented with an illuminated address by the club.

His debut in the senior team was eagerly anticipated and took place in August 1957 at White Hart Lane in front of an audience of more than 52,000. Certainly, they were not disappointed as Jimmy lived up to his reputation, and pre-match billing.

The press were unanimous in their acclaim. Typical was the comment, "Greaves entered the White Hart Lane scene with a schoolboy's reputation… his opportunities were limited. But who was not impressed by the second- half dribble which took him gliding past three challengers in six yards?" Almost

inevitably on that occasion he opened his scoring account in League football by creating, and finishing off, the late goal which gave Chelsea the draw they scarcely deserved.

A star had arrived on the big screen. Six goals from the opening nine games was an excellent start. Wisely, his manager, Ted Drake, saw fit to rest the youngster for a few weeks as the heavy grounds arrived, before unleashing him from the dressing-room on the morning of Christmas Day. Like a greyhound springing from its trap, he responded by scoring four times.

Many are the memories of those days. Up against the Wolves' trio of international defenders, Billy Wright, Ron Flowers and Bill Slater, he waltzed past them all at will to score five, leaving them bewildered and leaden-footed in the process. Twice more he 'went nap', against Preston North End, at Deepdale, and against West Bromwich Albion. Before his 21st birthday he had scored his century of goals.

Figures, in Jimmy's case, tell much of the story but many who never saw him must wonder at his methods. Lightly built, at 5ft 8ins and just over 10st, and even lighter on his feet, his ball-control was superb. A razor-sharp brain, allied to a wonderful sense of anticipation constantly kept him at least one move ahead of most defenders. Many of the goals he scored were simplicity itself, once his swift mental reactions had taken him into position for the final kill.

Of course, at times he did make spectacular strikes, too. His high speed dribbling could leave opponents trailing in his wake and, when faced by the goalkeeper after one of his surging runs, there was usually only one conclusion. Few could match the accuracy of Greaves' finishing.

Despite an 11th-hour bid by chairman Joe Mears to keep him at The Bridge, he was whisked off to Italy in 1961, ironically just at the moment the shackles of the maximum weekly wage for professional footballers in England was being removed. On what was, inevitably, an occasion highly-charged with emotion, he bade farewell to his Stamford Bridge fans in his last match for Chelsea in the most appropriate way he knew. By scoring four times.

Italy, and AC Milan, was never home for the boy from East Ham, and he returned to London 12 months later to sign for Tottenham Hotspur, despite another Chelsea attempt to lure him back. At White Hart Lane, fresh triumphs fell upon him as Spurs became one of the country's most successful, and most articulate, clubs of that era. Needless to say with Greaves in the side there was rarely a shortage of goals. Forty-four of them were scored in an England shirt, from 57 outings. A ratio seldom achieved in the international arena. Yet, controversially, Sir Alf Ramsey saw fit to dispense with his services in the latter stages of his successful 1966 World Cup Campaign.

Later he had problems in his personal life which, happily, were solved by outside help, and his own self-discipline, before his 'second career' as a television commentator introduced him to generations who were unlucky enough never to have marvelled at his genius as a player.

For, as the famous Wolverhampton Wanderers international player and manager, Stan Cullis, once said: "Jimmy Greaves was the greatest finisher of all time." A matter of fact, rather than opinion.

'The Doc' Brings His Remedy

TOMMY Docherty became the sixth manager in Chelsea's history in January 1962 after three months working with the first team in his capacity as chief coach. Already Drake's ailing team, some short of experience, and others too long in the tooth, and all low in morale, were virtually doomed to relegation. Even so, the former Scottish international immediately roared into action much as his predecessor had done nine years earlier, making his presence felt in the most positive way.

Strict discipline was imposed. Any miscreant was liable to find his wage packet savagely depleted.

New manager Tommy Docherty arrives at Stamford Bridge. Life would certainly never be predictable under The Doc.

Training was rigorous and highly organised. And those who could not, or would not, conform to the new regime were quickly shown the door. Throughout Docherty's reign, whatever else, life was never dull, or predictable. And, as a result, Chelsea's name was kept constantly in the sports headlines.

Two wins in November, one of them a 3-0 victory against Arsenal at Highbury, had suggested better things. But the team too rarely showed themselves capable of avoiding the drop back to the Second Division although, mathematically at least, hope was kept alive until Easter.

Meanwhile, Docherty was experimenting and giving youth its fling. In the process he also brought in the experienced and dependable Andy Malcolm (West Ham United) at wing-half back, and Welsh international centre-forward, Graham Moore. Peter Sillett, the lone survivor from the 1954-55 championship team, ended his Stamford Bridge career, along with brother John.

By the time the 1962-63 season started, Docherty's plans for the future had been laid. One major signing was full-back Eddie McCreadie, a Scot from East Stirlingshire, another, Frank Upton, a Drake investment from Derby County, became established at left-half, with John Mortimore, also aged 28, giving the team a much needed leavening of experience. Otherwise the emphasis remained firmly staked on the graduates still steadily emerging from the juniors.

Such as Peter Bonetti, Tambling and Bridges were joined on a regular basis by Ken Shellito, Terry Venables, Bert Murray and, later, Allan Harris, and the team, now responding to the new manager's constantly varying moods and methods, simply stormed their way to the top of the Second Division table, leaving opponents bewildered by their pace, skill and boundless enthusiasm. The 2-0 Boxing Day victory over Luton Town left them seven points clear of their nearest rivals, Bury. The spectre of Jimmy Greaves had at last been laid.

There was, however, one Chelsea tradition which Docherty had not bargained for, and that was the flare for inconsistency, which had bedevilled the club for more than half a century.

The first five months of the season included 17 wins as against four losses. Now came a run of five consecutive defeats, with only a single goal being scored. To be fair, this somersault in form coincided with the worst winter conditions experienced since 1947, causing a virtual

*Frank Upton scores the only goal of the game against Sunderland to give Chelsea what
proved to be a vital win, earlier in the season.*

*Sunderland's Charlie Hurley (facing) and Brian
Clough get between Chelsea's Peter Bonetti
(obscured) and Ken Shellito (2) during the game
at Stamford Bridge in September 1962. Chelsea
won 1-0 and continued their good start which
eventually ended in promotion back to the old
First Division. At the end of the season Chelsea
had pipped Sunderland for second place on goal
average.*

shut-down of football in Britain. Chelsea played no League fixtures in
January and only two in the first nine weeks of 1963. By the end of
March, Sunderland had knocked the Blues off their perch at the top of
the table and promotion was far from the certainty that it had seemed
three months earlier.

April brought about a partial revival, but it was the visit of Stoke
City to The Bridge on 11 May on which seemingly depended the
success – or failure – of the campaign. In front of 66,000, the team
from the Potteries, inspired and orchestrated by 48-year-old Stanley
Matthews, won that vital contest by the only goal scored. All was
nearly lost, but not quite.

The next stop, seven days later, was at Roker Park Sunderland, with
the Wearsiders still leading the table three points ahead of Chelsea,
who were, albeit with one less game played, in third position. It was
now that Docherty made what he described as 'the gamble of my life'.
Out from the side went Murray, Bridges and Moore. In came Derek
Kevan, recently signed from West Bromwich Albion, Frank Upton
who, for the first time was picked to play at centre-forward, and little
Tommy Harmer at the age of 34, having been signed after a long and

*Derek Kevan heads his only goal for Chelsea, in the 7-0 win over Portsmouth on the last day of the 1962-63 season. The landslide victory put
Chelsea back in the top flight.*

Chelsea's side which won promotion back to Division One in 1962-63. Back row (left to right): Venables, Upton, Bonetti, Mortimore, McCreadie, Shellito. Front row: Murray, Tambling, Bridges, Moore, Blunstone. Insets: Allan Harris, Kevan, Harmer.

The final act, appropriately, was to be staged at Stamford Bridge, with victory against Portsmouth needed to ensure promotion. On an early summer's evening, none of the drama of the previous fixture was repeated. Kevan's goal in the second minute of the match started a landslide. Tambling went on to score four times, Blunstone once, and a Venables penalty made it 7-0.

Docherty's sergeant-major approach had worked. His side, average age 21, had responded to his iron-fist discipline and gained his respect.

Back in the First Division, there were few changes in personnel. Kevan had moved out after seven games, never in harmony with his manager, and Ron Harris began his long and honourable career. Docherty was now assembling his own team and, such was his charisma, they would have been prepared to follow him anywhere.

Potentially, it was possibly the strongest line-up in the club's history. Peter Bonetti was little behind Gordon Banks as the best goalkeeper in the country. A solid looking defence was based on John Mortimore and Ron Harris

Peter Bonetti dives at the feet of Sheffield Wednesday's Tom McAnearney. The Owls won this game at Stamford Bridge in October 1963, 1-0.

honourable career with Tottenham Hotspur, to assist with coaching the younger players.

Miraculously the gamble paid off. Heavyweights Kevan and Upton pressurised Sunderland's defence, unused to such boisterous and questionable methods. And in fairy tale fashion, the only goal of the match was scored by Harmer, almost totally unaware of his achievement, as the ball was fortuitously deflected into the net off his left thigh. Chelsea, booed off the field, had won a gallant victory by methods even Docherty admitted afterwards had brought no great credit on him.

in the centre with the full-back partnership of Shellito and McCreadie generally considered already the best in the League.

In midfield Terry Venables, the tactical director, dictated the pattern of play, his astute passes constantly unhinging and cutting open opposition defences. At this time he was probably playing the best, and most influential, football of his career. Never short of ideas, or the initiative to put them into practice, unhappily he found himself increasingly in conflict with Docherty, each a strong personality, neither prepared to compromise.

July 1963, London swelters in a heatwave after one of the worst winters on record – and Chelsea manager Tommy Docherty talks tactics with his players who face a quick return to Division One.

John Mortimore heads clear from Spurs' Mel Hopkins during the 1963-64 season. Bobby Tambling (8) is the other Chelsea player.

And then, in the front line, Bobby Tambling, a lethal scorer of goals from either wing or through the centre, was on his way to becoming the most prolific marksman in Chelsea's history, with the speedy Barry Bridges and Bert Murray, able assistants. Murray's 17 goals from the wing in the 1964-65 season had only once been exceeded, by Spence 30 years earlier. Not the least of the attacking weapons was provided by Frank Blunstone's mazy and penetrative dribbles, often wrong-footing opposing defenders and leaving them trailing in his wake.

All the time others were emerging from the juniors, treading on the heals of those presently ahead in the queue. No one held a first-team place by divine right, all of Docherty's squad mindful of his unpredictability and ruthless make-up which could erupt without warning, and for the slightest reason.

Never in with a genuine chance of winning the Championship in 1963-64, from November onwards Chelsea remained comfortably tucked in behind the leading group of clubs. No mean achievement in view of the poverty of their performances in this division less than two years before. An early FA Cup exit at the hands of Huddersfield Town was one of the few blemishes in a season of notable progress.

By the following August, John Hollins had claimed the number-four shirt which he was to wear for 12 years, and Docherty added further strength to the squad with two shrewd transfer deals. Marvin Hinton, a dual purpose defender, equally at home at right-back or centre-half, came from Charlton Athletic, while George Graham was obtained from Aston Villa for 'a song', to partner Bridges in the centre of attack in order to allow Tambling to replace

Goalkeeper Lawrie Leslie is well beaten as Chelsea's Jimmy Murray scores his side's second goal against Stoke City at Stamford Bridge in October 1964. Chelsea won 4-0.

In January 1965, Chelsea met Northampton Town in the third round of the FA Cup and helped prepare for it with a visit to the International Boat Show at Earls Court where they showed the models who adorned the craft a thing or two about football. Goalkeeper Peter Bonetti (crouching) steadies the ball.

January 1966 and striker Peter Osgood (left) shares a joke with Chelsea boss Tommy Docherty and sportswriter Bernard Joy, the former Arsenal centre-half. This season, Osgood established himself with 37 senior appearances.

Blunstone on the left wing, his career prematurely and tragically terminated by injury.

By this time Docherty had appointed David Sexton as his coach and second in command. Totally different in temperament, his coaching skills and shrewd brain quickly gained him the confidence of his pupils and his unobtrusively quiet calming influence behind the scenes was another bonus.

So strong now was the playing staff that for much of the 1964–65 campaign it seemed as if the team could even pull off a 'treble', of Football League, FA Cup and Football League Cup, which, although it had been introduced in 1960, was only now becoming recognised as a major competition.

Chelsea led the table several times during the winter and were never out of touch with the top positions, but a 4–0 defeat by Manchester United at Old Trafford early in March, swiftly followed two weeks later, by elimination from the FA Cup at the hands of Liverpool, the first of three consecutive semi-finals in which Chelsea were to figure at Villa Park, left their season almost in tatters. Confidence was now severely shaken by the realisation that the necessary experience and maturity to handle such situations, in some cases, had still to be acquired.

Luck, too, had been against them in the semi-final when Mortimore's headed 'goal' was unaccountably disallowed. Maybe, also, Docherty's excitability and

Bobby Tambling
– Record Goalscorer

BOBBY Tambling first played for the Chelsea juniors in the 1957-58 season, immediately making his mark by scoring 33 goals from 25 games, a tally which included no fewer than seven hat-tricks, as well as five goals in a match against Southend United. One of the greatest names in Chelsea's history had announced his arrival in the most positive way, and along a route which he was to follow throughout his career.

As a 17-year-old he made his first-team debut in February 1959 against West Ham United, in front of a crowd of 53,000 at Stamford Bridge, alongside another newcomer Barry Bridges, also 17.

Fourteen minutes after the start he had scored his first goal in senior football, leaving the experienced full-back, John Bond, for dead along his path. More than 200 other goals were to follow. 'The Labourer's lad' from Hayling Island had arrived. "My legs feel as though I haven't stopped running for 24 hours," Tambling said afterwards. In fact, he was to spend more than 500 hours doing just that in his career at The Bridge.

Kept under wraps for almost another two years, he found himself taking over the main responsibility of planting the ball into the opponents' net, filling the gap which had existed since the departure of Jimmy Greaves to Italy.

Initially he operated, in conjunction with Barry Bridges, as a 'double spearhead', attacking down the centre. Later he was employed mainly along the left-hand flank, where he revelled in the more open spaces.

He once acknowledged his debt to Greaves. "I picked up a lot from Jimmy," he once said, "But it was no good setting myself up as another Greaves – I had to pursue my own style."

That style was based on a sudden acceleration, taking the shortest route to goal whenever possible, and a powerful left foot. Many of his goals were scored after spectacular dashes, at full speed on the run. Once his pace slackened as he approached the age of 30, so did his output of goals.

There were many memorable, golden moments. At Aston Villa in September 1966 he scored five times in Chelsea's 6-2 away victory, limping off the field after scoring the fifth, thereby missing the chance of equalling George Hilsdon's record of six in a match, set up 60 years earlier.

On three occasions he managed four goals in a match, and most famously on that unforgettable night at The Bridge in May 1963, when Portsmouth were demolished by a 7-0 victory which clinched Chelsea's promotion back to Division One. The evening was suitably capped when he proudly led his triumphant team into the director's box to receive the acclaim of some 55,000 fans.

Strangely, he won only three full international caps

for England, scoring one goal. At Under-23 level he made 13 appearances.

In January 1970 he left Stamford Bridge, no longer assured of his place in the first team as Dave Sexton's Chelsea were on the threshold of the most successful period of their history. For another eight years he contin-

ued to play the game he loved, first with Crystal Palace and then with three separate clubs in Ireland.

But his final bow at Chelsea was still to follow. On Saturday, 10 April 1971, as a member of the Palace side, he returned to Stamford Bridge to receive an illuminated address, putting on permanent record his 202 goals for the Blues, in 370 first-team matches – all scored before his 29th birthday. Not a bad achievement for someone who started so unpromisingly "After the first week as a groundstaff boy, I was nearly in tears with homesickness. But I decided to keep it to myself and battle it out."

George Graham and Allan Young of Chelsea worry the AS Roma goalkeeper during the Inter-Cities Fairs Cup tie at Stamford Bridge in September 1965. Chelsea won 4–1 and after a goalless draw in Rome went through to the second round.

AC Milan goalkeeper Balzarini saves from Bobby Tambling during the Inter-Cities Fairs Cup first round first leg game in Milan in February 1966.

lack of managerial experience meant that the repair of morale and self-belief would have been achieved more rapidly with a somewhat calmer and more conciliatory approach.

Be that as it may, some consolation was at hand when Chelsea beat Leicester City, 3-2 on aggregate in the two-legged League Cup Final, one of the goals a brilliant solo effort from McCreadie being the outstanding feature of two otherwise somewhat low-key performances.

Any hopes that this could give a kick-start for a late assault on the League championship, however, soon proved wide of the mark. Mathematically still very much in contention, defeat, again by Liverpool, in a 'four-pointer' at Stamford Bridge over Easter was a prelude to a most unfortunate disciplinary furore prior to Chelsea's penultimate fixture at Burnley.

What should have been dealt with internally as a domestic matter was blown out of all proportion by Docherty's impetuous, impulsive and insensitive handling of the affair, and his public humiliation of eight of his first-team players who broke curfew by returning to their Blackpool hotel in the early hours of the morning. Promptly, they were dispatched back to London by train with replacements hurriedly speeding northwards in the reverse direction. Inevitably this lead to defeat against Burnley at Turf Moor, and also in the final game, ironically enough at Blackpool. It was a sad epilogue to a wonderful season that so nearly was even more than that.

Before the curtain went up again, Docherty had taken 20 of his players, among them the unknown

Peter Osgood, for a month's tour of Australia, from which they returned unbeaten, before toning up for the rather sterner battles ahead with further visits to Germany, Sweden and Denmark.

At Stamford Bridge the vast and imposing west terracing had disappeared as the outlines of a new 9,500 capacity stand signalled the biggest ground development since Archibald Leitch planned his East Stand in 1905. So high were expectations that all season tickets had been sold.

No major changes had occurred on the playing staff but Dave Sexton had now begun his managerial career with Leyton Orient, and Jimmy Andrews, a Scot who had played for three London clubs, was appointed as his successor.

Without doubt, Chelsea were now regarded as London's most glamorous football club, on the verge of realising that potential foreseen by Gus Mears and Frederick Parker in those long ago Edwardian days.

Disappointingly, the team was never seriously in contention for the League championship, Liverpool maintaining a formidable lead from Christmas onwards, and a final sixth place was considered less than satisfactory.

To prevent fixture congestion Chelsea made the decision not to defend their Football League Cup in view of qualification for European competition. The Inter-Cities Fairs Cup was now more prestigious, and more highly organised, than when the Blues made an earlier brief appearance in 1958-59, with AC Milan, Barcelona, Standard Liege and Sporting Lisbon this time among the entrants. And immediately it caught

Peter Osgood sends in a diving header at the Wiener SC goal at Stamford Bridge. Chelsea won the second leg 2-1 to level the scores and then went through on the toss of a coin when the play-off was drawn after extra-time. They reached the semi-final before losing 5-0 to Barcelona in another play-off.

the imagination and attracted large crowds. With 36,000 terrace spaces available at four shillings (20p) and top-priced seats 15 shillings (75p), Chelsea's five home fixtures in that competition managed to bank over £100,000.

AS Roma provided the first opposition, a 4-1 victory in the first leg at Stamford Bridge virtually deciding the outcome, this game including the sending off of Eddie McCreadie. Seeming not to be particularly significant at the time, the repercussions in Rome a fortnight later were horrendous. Bottles, aimed at Chelsea players, were thrown on to the pitch, one of them hitting John Boyle, and after somehow holding out for a goalless draw their retreat to the airport was marked by further outbreaks of violence with the team coach, the primary target, suffering considerable damage.

After Wiener Sport-Club, from Austria, had been beaten in the second round, AC Milan were Chelsea's next opponents, a stunning goal from Osgood at The Bridge enabling the tie to be squared at 3-3, both teams winning their home fixtures, 2-1.

With such unwanted intrusions as penalty shoot-outs unheard of in those days, it was back to the San Siro Stadium for the third instalment, skipper Ron Harris losing the toss for the right to stage the match. But 'Chopper' was never one to accept defeat lightly, and when an epic play-off, ending in deadlock at 1-1, had still failed to separate the teams, Harris once more found himself in the guessing business. This time his correct call of 'heads' may have provided an unworthy conclusion to a memorable five and a half hour contest, but at least most neutral observers made Chelsea winners on merit. Docherty's team were fast learners and rapidly becoming 'streetwise'.

TSV München proved less of an obstacle, a 3-2

aggregate win providing a passport into the semi-final and a meeting with mighty CF Barcelona.

Despite so much solid achievement and so much progress within the club, rifts were beginning to appear between manager and certain players. Venables had masterminded his own tactical plan for the team in Rome six months earlier, successfully using Marvin Hinton as 'sweeper' to protect Chelsea's three-goal lead, with Docherty completely unaware of such scheming behind his back. McCreadie had become disillusioned and was openly expressing his dissatisfaction, and Bridges, also, was none too happy after returning from England's close-season tour to find his club place in jeopardy.

A two-goal deficit from the first semi-final leg in Barcelona's Nou Camp stadium was cancelled by a similar score in Chelsea's favour at The Bridge, both goals being attributed to Spanish defenders. But, after again failing to guess correctly in the toss for choice of venue, the third chapter ended decisively 5-0 in Barcelona's favour. McCreadie, Venables and Bridges were, significantly, among the absentees.

A month earlier Chelsea's FA Cup aspirations had again been halted in a Villa Park semi-final, 'underdogs' Sheffield Wednesday cantering home to a win, considerably easier than the 2-0 score suggested.

After the final whistle Docherty, unable to hide his feelings, was clearly furious. Chelsea's best team up to that time and, collectively, still some way short of their peak, was about to be broken up.

Venables was transferred to Spurs, Bridges and Murray to Birmingham City, and George Graham departed to Arsenal. The dissatisfaction of others was, in some cases, temporarily hidden beneath the fallen masonry. Even so, the damage which such wanton destruction caused was never wholly to be restored.

All Change Once More

ON 1 JULY 1966, whilst walking in a park in Oslo, Mr J.H.Mears, chairman of Chelsea FC since 1940, collapsed and died. As chairman of the Football Association he had accompanied the England team on their pre-World Cup tour to Finland and Norway.

The fourth chairman in Chelsea's 60-year-history, he was the most able and most highly respected, administrator in the game at that time. Certainly his loss was keenly felt at Stamford Bridge, where, in the increasingly turbulent Tommy Docherty era, his wisdom, poise and dignity were priceless qualities. A skilful arbitrator, a few well-chosen and quietly spoken words diffused many a potentially explosive situation. And, above all, he was a man Docherty knew he could trust and one of the few whom he respected.

His successor, Charles Pratt, a member of the board since 1935, and whose father had also been chairman for a short time, was a logical appointment but, unfortunately, never captured the confidence, or co-operation of his headstrong manager. It was a partnership never likely to endure or to exist harmoniously.

Docherty, too, had difficulties on his own account. His team had been partially dismantled at his own behest, and this was inevitably going to pose problems. Wounds, too, had been opened which only time could heal.

First among the newcomers was Charlie Cooke, who had already made his debut in the blue shirt against Barcelona the previous May. Whatever Docherty's shortcomings, he had an eye for unearthing rare talent, often in players yet to reveal their full potential. One such signing was Tommy Baldwin, arriving from Arsenal, in part-exchange for the greatly lamented departure of George Graham. Soon, fate had dealt an unexpected blow when Peter Osgood broke his leg at Blackpool in a League Cup fixture in the early weeks of the season.

Immediately, Docherty responded by shelling out £100,000 for Aston Villa's centre-forward, Tony Hateley, at 25 a proven goalscorer whose height and heading ability had invited a comparison, exaggerated

Chelsea in 1966, the season they achieved their longest winning sequence in League and Cup combined - eight games from 27 December to 12 February. Back row (left to right: John Hollins, Marvin Hinton, Peter Bonetti, Ron Harris, John Boyle, Eddie McCreadie, Joe Fascione. Front row: Barry Bridges, George Graham, Peter Osgood, Terry Venables, Bobby Tambling.

Arsenal goalkeeper Jim Furnell blocks a shot from Bobby Tambling at Stamford Bridge in September 1966. Chelsea won 3-1, on their way to finishing ninth in the First Division.

and unfair, with Tommy Lawton himself. In fact, the new giant scarcely fitted Chelsea's ball passing game and he was always likely to be a short-term investment.

Others, also, were making their mark. Among them Joe Kirkup, a stylish full-back from West Ham United, a successor to Shellito, tragically forced into premature retirement after four operations on his left knee, and who, almost certainly, would have been Sir Alf Ramsey's first choice as England's right-back for the 1966 World Cup winning team. John Boyle, after two seasons on the fringe of the first team, now established himself as an aggressive midfield terrier, whilst a third recruit was Jim Thomson a versatile defender, never a permanency in the side, but a reliable stand-in wherever required.

Unlike the previous three seasons, a serious challenge for the League championship never seemed likely, once Osgood's injury removed him from the action. At that stage, in early October, Chelsea led the table, one point ahead of Tottenham Hotspur. For a further month they maintained that position somewhat precariously before an eight-match spell without a win effectively ended any serious assault on the title. A final place of ninth was, at least, respectable and as good as could be expected in the circumstances.

League Cup progress was brought to a halt by Blackpool, in a replay at The Bridge, but it was in the FA Cup that the season really took off.

The first hurdle, against Huddersfield Town in the West Riding, was surmounted easily enough, and Brighton & Hove Albion were also accounted for, by four clear goals in a Stamford Bridge replay after a 1-1 draw at the Goldstone Ground. Two home draws in the fifth and sixth rounds against the Sheffield clubs eliminated, in turn, United (1-0) and Wednesday (2-0) to provide a passport into another Villa Park semi-final, this time against Don Revie's rapidly emerging Leeds United.

Whereas at the same stage in the competition two years earlier, a hotly-disputed refereeing decision had deprived Chelsea of what most people considered a perfectly legitimate goal, now the position was reversed.

With Chelsea precariously hanging on to a precious one goal lead in injury time, Peter Lorimer sent a free-kick, awarded for an infringement a few feet outside the penalty area, powerfully past Peter Bonetti's despairing dive, only for the referee to rule that he had not blown his whistle for the kick to be taken. Gratefully, Chelsea accepted such a fortunate reprieve and Lorimer's second effort was cleared – seconds before the end of a hard-fought contest.

Earlier, Tony Hateley's goal, a powerful header from Cooke's cross, was the big man's most telling contribution during his ten-month stay at The Bridge. Even so there was to be no happy ending at Wembley.

Left: Chelsea and Tottenham players are guests of honour at a dinner held at the Hilton Hotel three days before the 1967 FA Cup Final. The dinner was given by the Anglo-American Sporting Club. Above: Chelsea players' wives outside Stamford Bridge on the eve of the 1967 FA Cup Final.

Tommy Baldwin and Tottenham's Dave Mackay in a battle for the ball at Wembley. It was Chelsea's first appearance in an FA Cup Final at the Empire Stadium and ended in a 2-1 defeat.

Former Chelsea stars at the 1967 FA Cup Final banquet. Back row (left to right): Andy Wilson (1923-31), George Mills (1929-43), Billy Russell (1927-36). Front row: Nils Middelboe (1913-21), Bob Thomson (1913-22), B.Howard Baker (1921-26).

Tottenham Hotspur dominated throughout the Final, in a game well short of the quality expected. Rarely in trouble, Spurs were cantering home as they entered the straight until a late Bobby Tambling goal gave the score-sheet a degree of respectability Chelsea scarcely deserved. The presence of Jimmy Greaves and Terry Venables in the opposition was no consolation either, in fact very much the reverse.

Meanwhile, problems off the field were steadily escalating. Rows between chairman and manager were constantly in the headlines. Equally, discontent in the dressing-room revealed further cracks in the edifice. One source of dissatisfaction regarded the players' Cup Final ticket distribution – at one stage 18 of them were angrily demanding transfers. It was scarcely the ideal preparation for a Cup Final.

Also rearing its ugly head was the question of the

renewal of the Stamford Bridge lease due in 1968, and complicated by the joint occupancy of the football club with the SB Greyhound Company which prevented the purchase of the freehold, a saga which was to drag on for another 25 years.

The 1967-68 season began with expectation lower than for several years. Incidents on Chelsea's summer tour in the Caribbean had led to Docherty being suspended from football management for 28 days by the Football Association, and this coincided with the manager's almost inevitable resignation on 6 October.

For at least the previous 12 months it had become clear that any hope of an armistice between board and manager, and manager and players, had long since been jettisoned by personality clashes, and by Docherty's uncompromising attitude. What had started five years before as an ideal marriage now ended in acrimonious divorce amid accusation and counter-accusation. It was indeed a sorry end to a chapter which had achieved so much, and promised so much more.

After a 17-day interregnum, during which time assistant manager Ron Suart stepped into the breach, Mr Pratt announced the appointment of Dave Sexton as Docherty's successor. "We are delighted to have him back. Indeed, when he left us three seasons ago, we did not want to lose him. In the meantime, we always regarded him with affection and we regard him as the best man in the world to do the job for which he has come back to Stamford Bridge."

With Chelsea already in the lower reaches of the First Division table and eliminated from the League Cup at the first attempt, there was clearly much repair work urgently required and Sexton quickly revealed his hand.

Totally different in almost every way from his

Tommy Docherty talks to his Chelsea team at Cheshunt in August 1967, on the eve of a new season. Two months later he was replaced by Dave Sexton.

Dave Sexton arrives to take over the manager's job at Stamford Bridge in October 1967.

predecessor, he immediately gained his players' respect and confidence. Indeed, a deputation from the dressing-room had previously recommended his appointment. Shy, retiring, and an introvert, with a shrewd brain and a high reputation following his earlier stays at Chelsea, and later with Leyton Orient and Arsenal, he was to prove an inspired choice.

Soon his influence was demonstrated. From Christmas onwards, 22 League fixtures produced 32 points and catapulted the team up the table from 18th position to a final placing of sixth. A promising FA Cup sequence of three victories was ended only by 1-0 defeat at the hands of Birmingham City after a somewhat dour encounter in the Midlands.

Already the team was being reshaped. Signings included the rugged defenders, David Webb (Southampton) and John Dempsey (Fulham). Alan Birchenall (Sheffield United) came to add weight and goalscoring potential whilst, later, Ian Hutchinson was to prove a marvellous bargain for £5,000, unearthed from non-League Cambridge United. Meanwhile, Peter Houseman was steadily staking his claim for a regular first-team place and the name of a certain Alan Hudson was constantly on the lips of those who watched the Chelsea juniors.

In eight months, Sexton had restored the club's credibility and was bringing in the tools required for the job of winning major trophies. Almost as important, his ship was sailing into calmer waters.

Peter Bonetti
– Poetry in Motion

COMPARISONS are inevitably odious and controversial and, certainly in football, can never reach a definite or satisfying conclusion. Peter Bonetti is the almost universal choice for the accolade of 'Chelsea's best-ever goalkeeper', and the number of people who would put forward the claims of such as Victor Woodley, for example, as an alternative contender are now a dwindling and less vocal band.

Not to be disputed, however, is that Bonetti fits well into a dynasty of top-class Chelsea goalkeepers, initiated by Willie Foulke and continuing, virtually unbroken, through Howard Baker, Woodley, John Jackson, Reg Matthews,

and, later to Eddie Niedzwiecki .

It was an auspicious day when Peter's mother wrote the letter to Chelsea, requesting a trial for her son. Not only did it settle his career, but it helped to construct the most successful, and colourful period of the club's history.

Nicknamed 'The Cat' for his extraordinary agility in the juniors in 1958, he never looked back. Like Ron Harris, whose career often ran parallel to Bonetti's, he began with an FA Youth Cup winners' medal, in 1960, having already made his first-team debut weeks earlier, deputising for Matthews and Robertson, both of whom were injured. Indeed, so impressively did he perform that he kept his position not only for the rest of that season but, with one break, for another 19 years.

Throughout this time he was probably the most consistent goalkeeper in the game. Many recall his outstanding games and countless brilliant saves.

Equally relevant for the teams he played in was his utter dependability as the seasons continued to roll by. Very rarely did he fall below the high standards he had set for himself. Countless deputies at Stamford Bridge lost heart, and patience, and moved elsewhere, unwilling to have their own careers stifled by a man they could never hope to emulate, or succeed.

His handling, particularly of high balls, was exemplary. He would pluck the ball out of the air with confident certainty, seemingly unaware of oncoming physical challenges from heavier built opponents. He commanded the goal area, his judgment in coming off his line superb. So, too, was his anticipation. And everything he did was achieved with gracefulness and poise.

In almost any other era, or in any other country, he would have made a much greater impression in international football. First, he lived in the shadow of Ron Springett and then was forced to play second fiddle to Gordon Banks. Seven appearances with the senior England team was a poor reward and, more unfortunately, it is for one indifferent game in the 1970 Mexico World Cup that he is best, and somewhat unfairly, remembered at this highest level in the game.

He was between the posts on all Chelsea's greatest occasions in the 1960s and 1970s; a vital member of all three major Cup-winning teams.

Perhaps his finest hour came on that golden April evening of 1970 at Old Trafford in the FA Cup Final replay. Who will ever forget those agonising moments, after an accidental collision with a Leeds United forward? Trainer Harry Medhurst, himself a member of the 'goalkeepers union', tended to his visibly swelling left knee for what seemed an eternity, before 'The Cat', looking anything but cat-like, gingerly resumed his post, scarcely able to put weight on to his left foot. Within minutes he was picking the ball from his net. But, bravely masking his handicap, he proceeded to make notable saves as the shots rained in. After Chelsea had taken the lead in extra-time, his goal became a fortress, the bombardment coming from every conceivable angle. But never once did Chelsea's severely handicapped goalkeeper flinch or falter.

Twelve months later, returning to the team after nearly three months absence through injury, it was yet another crucial save in Athens, against Real Madrid in the Cup-winners' Cup Final, which saved Chelsea's bacon.

Having extended his Stamford Bridge career past his 37th birthday, he played, briefly, with Dundee United before turning his attention to coaching goalkeepers. Three England managers, in turn, installed him in their coaching squad on a permanent basis, a tribute to his skill and lasting reputation.

The FA Cup At Last

DAVE Sexton, as he knew full well, had inherited a club whose ills were deep-seated. Festering sores needed time to heal fully and there was to be no quick fix. The new manager, with time on his side, was content to assess the situation and bide his time.

Chairman Charles Pratt had died in March 1968 and had been succeeded by his deputy, Leonard Withey. However, at least expectations were high amongst the fans, as was proved by the new record receipts for season tickets. There were no new signings on parade, although two names, destined to play a major role in Chelsea's future, had been added to the pay-roll.

Ian Hutchinson was being given time to find his bearings in unfamiliar surroundings by finding his feet in reserve-team football. Alan Hudson, having served a two-year apprenticeship with the juniors, was now in his first season as a full-time professional, and already displaying outstanding talent. But he, too, was left under wraps for the time being.

After the hectic carryings-on of the Docherty days there were few high points in the 1968-69 season. Chelsea maintained a respectable League position just behind the leading group of clubs, only two defeats in the final 14 fixtures giving a promise of still better things to come.

Disappointingly, neither Cup competition brought lasting joy. A sixth-round FA Cup defeat against West Bromwich Albion at Stamford Bridge being a

Arsenal's Bob Wilson grabs a high ball as Tommy Baldwin rushes in with Gunners' defender Bob McNab getting in between. A Peter Houseman goal gave Chelsea victory in this game at Highbury in November 1968.

Ron Harris
— The Chelsea Chopper

It is most unlikely that any future Chelsea player will approach Ron Harris' tally of 795 first-team appearances. Apart from the ability to maintain peak form for nigh on 20 years, at the highest level, other qualities, too, are called for. Fitness, consistency, dedication, self-discipline and club loyalty come high up on any such list. And Ron, or 'Chopper' as he will always be remembered, had all those in good measure.

Harris first came to Chelsea's notice, along with elder brother Allan, in the late 1950s and early '60s. They were members of a rich vintage of club juniors who won the FA Youth Cup in 1960 and 1961. By the time Docherty's resurgent team stormed its way to promotion from the Second Division in the spring of 1963, Ron already had a handful of senior appearances under his belt and was ready for the challenge of playing against the country's top opposition.

From August 1963 until May 1980 he was an essential part of the first-team furniture. Often overshadowed by stars whose lights dazzled more brightly, he was virtually never absent from his post somewhere in the back of the defence, his game seemingly immune from the vagaries of form which affect less resilient mortals.

Ron was versatile enough to slot, more or less, into any position in the back four, or even to adopt a withdrawn role in midfield. Even if his lack of inches prevented him from possessing aerial dominance, he was nevertheless an ideal partner for such as John Mortimore, John Dempsey or Micky Droy in central defence. Right-back was probably his more natural habitat, where he could better utilise the stronger of two good feet.

His strength in the tackle was, of course, his trademark, many opponents deciding to opt out of confrontation. Frequently, he would be detailed to shadow an opponent whose

threat had been identified by his manager. In this role he could render some of the biggest names in football, ineffective and impotent, so endearing were his attentions. And if his passing was less memorable than most of his other attributes, his astute brain and tactical awareness were always alive for an opportunity to turn defence into attack.

Sadly, if perhaps understandably, his medals were all won in the domestic game. The FA Youth Cup in 1961, the Football League Cup in 1965, FA Cup in 1970 and the European Cup-winners' Cup in 1971. 'Chopper' was on parade on each occasion.

Four under-23 appearances were as close as he came to full international recognition, the England managers of his time being, perhaps, put off by his uncomplicated approach and methods which, at times, did not meet with the approval of referees. A not altogether fair judgement.

After his years at, and on, The Bridge during which he savoured both high success and the low-water marks of relegation in 1975 and 1979, Ron wound down, briefly, with Brentford, as player-coach, and at Aldershot whom he managed for six months, before later becoming involved in a possible takeover of that club in time of crisis.

Perhaps disillusioned by the direction in which the game was moving, he turned away from football altogether, however, to make an outstanding success in the leisure business in the heart of rural Wiltshire.

But to football, and Chelsea, he gave his all. Once asked by a reporter what he would do if he won the jackpot on the football pools, his reply was typical. "Make sure I reported for training on time next day", came the reply.

February 1969 and Stamford Bridge lies quiet under a blanket of snow. That afternoon's FA Cup tie against Stoke City was postponed.

Bobby Tambling tries to hook the ball back over the head of Burnley goalkeeper Thomson at Stamford Bridge in April 1969. The other Burnley player is Latcham. Chelsea lost 3-2 but eventually managed a creditable fifth place in Division One.

Peter Osgood scores Chelsea's first goal against Everton at Stamford Bridge in November 1969, hammering the ball past Gordon West.

particularly unexpected set-back. Bobby Tambling was now in his final season as a regular first-teamer, for the fifth time finding his name at the head of the goalscorer's list, with his 17 League goals one ahead of Tommy Baldwin's total.

In fact many will remember the season best for a happening which, even measured by Chelsea's standards, was somewhat macabre. A fourth-round FA Cup replay against Preston North End was apparently meandering to its close, with Chelsea 2-0 ahead and a quarter of an hour remaining, when Stamford Bridge was plunged into darkness. The floodlights had failed due to a fire in the main electrical junction box, much too grave a matter for immediate surgery.

But that was only the first instalment of the story. Reassembling for the re-run five days later, it was now North End who found themselves in the lead by a

Eddie McCreadie gets the ball away from Arsenal's Peter Marinello at Highbury in January 1970. Chelsea enjoyed a 3-0 win over the Gunners and would eventually finish third in Division One. But it was the FA Cup which would lead to real glory that season.

single goal, with 60 seconds to go. Tony Waddington, manager of Stoke City, who were due to meet the winners of the tie later that same week, had already left to catch his train home and to lay plans for his team's visit to Preston. Arriving in Staffordshire, he was somewhat disconcerted to learn that Chelsea goals by David Webb, and Charlie Cooke, deep into injury time, had upset his calculations.

On the surface, Sexton's first season had seemed to do little more than keep the pot bubbling. In effect, his shrewd scheming for the future was vastly more ambitious than it appeared at the time.

Again in 1969-70, he was happy with the talent available on the staff and, apart from Paddy Mulligan, a no-nonsense and versatile Irish defender signed in October, there were no newcomers of note. Chelsea never at anytime appeared likely champions, the Merseyside duo, together with Leeds United and Derby County, setting a hot pace as front runners. And, in truth, much of the flair and somewhat wayward genius in the Blues' ranks was always more likely to blossom on the big occasion, and most especially in knock-out football. And so it proved.

The shock defeat, on a wintry October night, in the fifth round of the League Cup in Carlisle may even have acted as the spur when the more prestigious FA Cup competition began three months later.

Birmingham City were disposed of with a minimum of fuss at the first hurdle, the much-feared striking twins, Osgood and Hutchinson, sharing the goals. Burnley proved a stiffer hurdle fighting back, late on, from a two-goal deficit at Stamford Bridge to force an uninviting replay in Lancashire. And, indeed, what a battle royal that challenge proved. Alan Hudson hit a post. Burnley then took a lead which they kept until 18 minutes from time, only for Peter Houseman to score probably the most spectacular goal of his career, hammering the ball into the corner of the net from outside the penalty area. The nearest either side could get to scoring after that was when Ian Hutchinson hit the bar. So to extra-time.

With Ron Harris man-marking, and man-handling, Burnley's Ralph Coates, who earlier had caused problems to Chelsea's defenders, first Baldwin, and then Houseman, the man of the match, scored precious goals with fog almost obliterating the final stages of an epic struggle.

The victory in the fifth round at Crystal Palace was more convincing, Osgood starting a landslide before half-time, briefly disturbed by a Palace equaliser which never threatened to stop the Chelsea bandwagon. The final score of 4–1 being a just reward for an impressive afternoon's work.

Next stop on the Wembley trail was Queen's Park Rangers, and Terry Venables, who were quite unable to prevent Chelsea putting on a marvellous exhibition of skilful play on the difficult, muddy, surface. A 4–2 scoreline in no way truly reflected Chelsea's superiority, emphasised by Osgood's hat-trick.

The reward was a semi-final draw against Third Division Watford at White Hart Lane, almost too good to be true. At long last was Chelsea's name already on the Cup? The Hertfordshire side proved themselves game competitors by equalising an early David Webb goal. But the final 5–1 margin of victory was the biggest in any FA Cup semi-final for 31 years.

In the other semi-final Don Revie's fearsome Leeds United overcame Manchester United and so the Wembley stage was set for an epic struggle. Twelve days before the great day, fate dealt Chelsea a cruel blow. In a rearranged League fixture at West Bromwich, Alan Hudson tore his ankle ligaments and was at once ruled out of what would, up to then, have been the most important game of his life. Throughout the season he had been quite outstanding, his creative play from midfield inviting favourable comparisons with anyone who had occupied his position throughout Chelsea's history.

Cleverly Sexton rearranged his team to accommodate replacement, Tommy Baldwin, by no means a straight swap for Hudson. Leeds were already the clear favourites, few experts apart from Geoffrey Green of *The Times*, seriously fancying the 'old unpredictables'.

The Wembley surface, belying its reputation, was in no fit state to stage any football match let alone a Cup Final. A recent horse-riding event had left its traditional billiard-table surface a mass of ruts and ridges on which good football could scarcely be expected. Certainly Leeds' opening goal would normally have been cleared off the line by McCreadie had the ball not skidded under his foot into the net rather than bouncing in the normal way. Thankfully, for

Above: Leeds are happy, Chelsea not so. Jack Charlton has just scored his side's first goal in the 1970 FA Cup Final at Wembley. Below: Chelsea's defence can only look in anguish as Mick Jones restores Leeds United's Wembley lead. But a second equaliser, from Ian Hutchinson, meant that Chelsea lived to fight another day.

Chelsea, the Leeds goalkeeper, Gary Sprake, soon fumbled a simple effort from Houseman to allow Chelsea a fortunate equaliser.

Apart from the eccentricities of the pitch, the main problem for the Blues was little Eddie Gray the Leeds winger, whose footwork and trickery left poor David Webb ruthlessly exposed time and again. And so dominant were the Yorkshiremen that their second goal, savagely rocketed past Bonetti by Mick Jones, seemed certain to be conclusive. But not quite. Against all probability and, almost before Leeds could regroup, there was Hutchinson producing Chelsea's second equaliser, heading in from Hollins' corner.

Extra-time was never likely to provide a result, the infamous surface already having extracted every ounce of energy from weary limbs in the preceding 90 minutes.

Never before since the opening of Wembley Stadium in 1923 had a replay been required in an FA Cup Final and, thankfully for the players at any rate, the second game was arranged for Old Trafford.

Peter Bonetti blocks a shot from Mick Jones at Wembley.

Sexton, in the meantime, made one vital tactical adjustment. Ron Harris was moved from his position at the heart of the defence to assume responsibility for policing Gray, a task which he had performed successfully many times in such situations – even Stanley Matthews on one occasion being reduced to a relatively mundane level by his personal attentions. Equally, Webb's switch to the centre was much more to his liking, and strength.

In many ways, the second match ran a course similar to the earlier contest. Once more Leeds found

Bonetti gets up high to collect the ball with Leeds' Jack Charlton still flat-footed at Old Trafford.

Inset: Peter Osgood dives to head Chelsea level in the Old Trafford replay. Main picture: Chelsea players mob Peter Osgood after his equaliser against Leeds.

themselves in the lead. Again Chelsea responded, through Peter Osgood's equaliser, which, this time, seemed to leave their opponents shaken, morale badly jolted.

John Hollins, Charlie Cooke and Osgood, himself, slowing the game more to the pace of their choice began to impose their skill and artistry, allowing them to dictate matters and achieve a measure of control on the proceedings hitherto lacking. Osgood's goal, in fact, following a clever inter-passing movement with Cooke, in retrospect, was a considerable psychological blow, apart from its mathematical importance.

Extra-time always seemed likely to produce a result on this occasion, after both trainers had used the time available to retune tiring limbs for one last-ditch effort. As it was, Chelsea's Harry Medhurst had already more than played his part early on by attending to Peter Bonetti's knee, alarmingly swollen following an accidental clash with a Leeds forward. Typically, the goalkeeper soldiered on still in considerable pain, but concealing his discomfort and reduced agility from the enemy.

If by no means a secret, Chelsea had one weapon which had often set up goals and scoring chances. Ian Hutchinson, his arms whirling, could propel his throw-ins from the touch-line deep into the penalty area and beyond, the trajectory of the ball often proving even more of a problem than its very range. And now, seconds before the end of the first period of extra-time, he demonstrated just how deadly this weapon could be.

Over came the ball, brushing Jack Charlton's head *en route*, before David Webb, with perfect timing, headed the ball powerfully inches inside the angle of post and crossbar.

Instantly Old Trafford was transformed into a sea of blue. Stranger embraced stranger. Some unashamedly shed tears of joy. Few seemed mindful of the crucial 15 minutes still to come.

There were alarms. There were moments when time stood still and heartbeat stopped. Marvin Hinton replaced Osgood to shore up the heroic defence until, after what seemed an age, referee Jennings ultimately brought the proceedings to an end and joy, unconfined at one end of the stadium contrasted starkly with the utter despair at the other.

Fifty-five years earlier Chelsea had returned to the Fulham Road from their first FA Cup Final, defeated and downcast as the clouds of war darkened the skies. Now it was back to scenes of wild, joyous celebration as, 24 hours later, an open-topped bus

David Webb jumps high above the Leeds defence to give Chelsea a dramatic victory in the 1970 FA Cup Final replay.

Eddie McCreadie makes a hefty clearance with Bonetti on the ground behind him.

Peter Osgood
— Wayward Genius

"PETER Osgood is one of those natural players a manager hopes and prays for throughout his career, but so rarely has his prayers answered." So wrote Peter's first manager at Chelsea, Tommy Docherty.

The 1960s produced several other kindred spirits in the game among them Rodney Marsh, Stan Bowles, and, of course, George Best. Players who made everything they did on a football field seem so easy, so natural. At times Osgood could appear casual, disinterested, his concentration wandering. Then, in a flash of sheer genius, he would produce a match-winning goal, with a shuffle, or a shift, taking him past opponents as if they did not exist.

Most usually, it was the big occasion which would bring the best out of Peter. Not for him those wet, gale-swept nights in the north country when he was asked to perform in an unimportant match in front of a few hardy huddles of hostile supporters. Rather, he preferred, and flourished on, the better-known platforms in the glare of the bright footlights.

Many were his memorable goals scored in a blue shirt. His crucial diving header in the 1970 FA Cup Final replay at Old Trafford; his two goals in the contests with Real Madrid in the Final of the European Cup-winners' Cup in Athens; a fabulous effort in a Fairs Cup-tie against AC Milan at Stamford Bridge, when a subtle feint sent an opponent the wrong way as he let fly with a left-footed missile which the Italian goalkeeper could never have seen; or a similar effort against Arsenal in a FA Cup-tie. Every supporter from those years will carry his own treasured memories.

It was frequently said that he was difficult to handle. Certainly he did not always conform, or see why he should. His sense of humour was not necessarily shared by those in authority. For Osgood life existed outside a football pitch and he intended to enjoy it and live it to the full, even, if, looking back, he may have had cause to regret some of his more impulsive actions which made a mockery of the stricter, inflexible, standards of discipline.

Certainly he was shunned by Sir Alf Ramsey, England's manager during most of his career. Four full international caps for his country was a scandalously poor reward for his great skills, his all-round talent, and artistry. But as he himself once wrote of Ramsey: "He wants hard work, lots of effort. Players who will run for each other, challenge back for the ball if they lose it. that's not my game. I'd very much like to play that way. But I can't. I've tried."

As age brought increasing weight and loss of speed Osgood's star quality went into decline. Much too soon, in March 1974, he was allowed to move to Southampton as Chelsea's most successful team fell apart at the seams. And when, in a desperate gamble, Danny Blanchflower, brought him back home, at the age of 31, it was too late. The magic had gone. He found himself surrounded by minnows where before there had been giants. Without support, he foundered. The old artist could never become mere labourer.

Better by far, to remember his great days on great occasions when he was virtually without par as an entertainer. Few players in Chelsea's long history have given greater pleasure.

It's ours! Skipper Ron Harris is carried aloft with the FA Cup after Chelsea's great win over Leeds in one of the most memorable Finals in recent memory.

Chelsea in 1970, the year of their famous FA Cup exploits. Back row (left to right): Marvin Hinton, Ian Hutchinson, David Webb, Tommy Hughes, Peter Bonetti, John Dempsey, Eddie McCreadie and John Hollins. Front row: Alan Birchenall, Charlie Cooke, Alan Hudson, John Boyle, Ron Harris, Peter Houseman, Peter Osgood, Tommy Baldwin and Bobby Tambling.

Happy homecoming. Ron Harris and Peter Bonetti hold up the FA Cup as it is paraded through the streets of Chelsea in April 1970.

bore its heroes, and their trophy, to the Hammersmith and Fulham Town Hall, amid vociferous cheers and singing. A long-forgotten music-hall song, mockingly entitled *When Chelsea won the Cup* was now supplanted by *Blue is the Colour.*

A European Crown –
And A Return To The Dark Days

NEVER before had Chelsea started any season with such a feeling of buoyant optimism as in August 1970. "We look forward to new heights, not only in our domestic competitions but in Europe", announced chairman Brian Mears, now in his second year of office and maintaining his family's dynasty.

Losing the FA Charity Shield fixture against Everton before the official start of the season was not an ideal beginning and, once again, the failure to puncture the points gap behind the front-runners in the League marathon reinforced the opinion that it was the 'sudden-death' occasions which brought out the best in Chelsea.

The only signing of note was Keith Weller, Millwall's London-born striker whom Sexton used, almost exclusively, wide on the right flank, in general opinion not his best position. A final sixth place was about par for the course, even if it did not reflect the ability of a very strong first-team squad. In contrast to many previous seasons, however, it was noticeable that of the nine defeats only two were at the hands of teams below them in the table. At least the maddening tradition of 'beating the best but falling to the lesser brethren' had been jettisoned.

By the third week in January, Chelsea's interest in both domestic Cup competitions was over. Manchester proved the insurmountable hurdles, United winning the League Cup clash at Old Trafford (no triumphant return), 2-1, and, more ignominiously, City walloping three goals past Peter Bonetti in a fourth-round FA Cup meeting at The Bridge.

Much different was the European Cup-winners' Cup venture. The first two hurdles provided little difficulty. The Greek side Aris Thessalonikis (6-2 on aggregate) and the Bulgarians, CFKA Sofia, were eliminated without alarms before Christmas.

In August 1970, Chelsea lost 2-1 at Stamford Bridge to League champions Everton in the FA Charity Shield game. Here Gordon West, the Everton goalkeeper, clears from David Webb. Other players are Joe Royle, Howard Kendall and Ian Hutchinson.

John Hollins gets in his shot as Bob Wilson and Bob McNab close in on him at Stamford Bridge in August 1970. The ball hit the crossbar and rebounded to Hollins, who followed up to score. Chelsea beat Arsenal 2-1.

But RFC Bruges were a different proposition. In Belgium, conceding two first-half goals was not an ideal start and, despite shutting the door after half-time, it still left a stiff task to be faced at Stamford Bridge. However, not only was this accomplished, but in the most forthright and dramatic fashion. As one writer put it, it was 'among the great occasions in the history of football played at Stamford Bridge'.

Peter Houseman's early goal was the ideal start but it was not until nine minutes from the end, and in an atmosphere of almost unbearable tension, that Peter Osgood stabbed the ball into the net from close range to buy a further 30 minutes of extra-time, during which Tommy Baldwin and Osgood, again, scored further goals to win a famous victory still fondly remembered and discussed by many in the 45,000 crowd on that unforgettable night.

Ironically, it was Manchester, again, for the semi-

Top, left: Manchester City's Colin Bell scores in the fourth-round FA Cup tie at Stamford Bridge in January 1971, when Chelsea went down 3-0. Harris, Webb and Hinton look on as Bonetti is well beaten. Top, right: Chelsea goalkeeper John Phillips goes to his left watched by Alan Hudson and the diving Peter Storey of Arsenal at Highbury in April 1971. The Gunners won 2-1 on their way to the

Keith Weller airborne against Manchester City in the European Cup-winners' Cup semi-final second leg in April 1971.

final, against City, but, this time, in an atmosphere entirely lacking in the tension of the previous year, two 1-0 victories being chiselled out against a team badly hit by injuries, and much lacking in confidence.

For the Final it was back to Greece for a confrontation with the mighty Real Madrid, perhaps not the force of their earlier invincible days, despite the presence in their ranks of the venerable Gento, a last link with the era of Di Stefano and Puskás, but still containing some formidable successors.

The Karaiskaki Stadium, predictably, contained the usual faithful army of Chelsea supporters, undeterred

Weller streaks in to head past the airborne Healy, only to see Manchester City's Tony Book head off the line. Chelsea won both legs of the Cup-winners' Cup semi-final by 1-0.

Peter Houseman challenges a Real Madrid player in the European Cup-winners' Cup Final in Athens in May 1971.

Suddenly, with Charlie Cooke the architect of an inspired move, it all changed. The Scotsman had chosen the occasion to exhibit some of his best football skills. Holding the ball, slowing the pace, his pass found John Boyle on the wing and the resultant cross was firmly met by Osgood, who easily beat Real's goalkeeper, Borja. With Cooke constantly continuing to catch the eye, the Spaniards were, even so, by no means finished and, after severe pressure on Bonetti's goal, they finally pierced his defence, a miskick by John Dempsey providing the excuse they needed to equalise.

Extra-time was a nerve-wracking affair with the heroics of Chelsea's defenders, not least Bonetti, Webb and Boyle, earning a replay.

by such minor considerations as distance and finance, and for some time it seemed as if they were due for disappointment. It was the Spaniards who made the early running, drawing on their great tradition, and experience, to produce some high quality football.

Before this took place, 48 hours later, Chelsea suffered a savage blow, with John Hollins being ruled out by injury. Once again, Sexton's tactical expertise was called into play. Cooke was withdrawn to perform a

Top: Chelsea players on their lap of honour after the Cup-winners' Cup triumph in Athens.

Middle: Hudson, Bonetti and Boyle with the Cup-winners' Cup.

deeper role in midfield, with Tommy Baldwin joining Osgood in attack, to allow more options and a greater fluidity.

Against all pre-match predictions, Chelsea found themselves two goals in the lead after half an hour. John Dempsey, a rare name on the score-sheet at the best of times, chose this ideal occasion to score a priceless opening goal and then Osgood, fastening on to a through pass from Baldwin, shimmied his way past a defender to score the second. Cooke was again a hero, with Alan Hudson also revelling in the atmosphere, and on a stage, ideal for his often unpredictable genius.

But all was by no means over. Real reduced the deficit with a quarter of an hour remaining during which time Bonetti was called upon to make a save as important and breath-taking as any in his long career, while David Webb prevented another shot from entering the net with an equally typical piece of anticipation and bravery.

Within 48 hours of the final whistle, the scene of 12 months earlier was being re-enacted in West London. The now familiar open-top bus, another trophy aloft, was snaking its way through the vast throng of delirious fans.

On the surface, the future seemed to hold the promise of still more, and possibly greater, triumphs. A £2 million new East Stand was on the drawing-board, merely the first stage in a scheme designed to make Stamford Bridge a 60,000 all-seater stadium, capable of enlargement to hold 80,000 spectators overall.

But, Dave Sexton was now faced with problems which were beginning to surface. Ian Hutchinson had not recovered from the serious knee injury which had caused him to miss much of the previous season. Keith Weller, through no fault of his own, was something of a misfit and there were the first signs of personality clashes between manager and certain of his players.

The 1971-72 season started poorly, with three League defeats in the

John Hollins takes the ball past Åtvidabergs Sten-ake Andersson in the Cup-winners' Cup second-round second leg game at Stamford Bridge in November 1971. The holders went out on the away-goals rule.

David Webb challenges Norwich City goalkeeper Kevan Keelan in the League Cup quarter-final tie at Carrow Road in November 1971. Chelsea eventually went through thanks to an Osgood goal.

Bonetti collects the ball with Webb and Osgood close by during the 1972 League Cup Final against Stoke City at Wembley. The Potters won 2-1.

Peter Osgood hits home Chelsea's goal against Stoke City in the 1972 League Cup Final.

opening four fixtures and it was again clear that Chelsea were not equipped to be serious contenders for the championship. New arrivals included Steve Kember, a tough and resourceful midfield player from Crystal Palace, and Chris Garland, bustling and enthusiastic in attack.

The first major upset occurred when the little-known Swedish side, Åtvidaberg, knocked Chelsea out of the European Cup-winners' Cup 1-1, on the 'away-goals rule'. Ironically, in the previous round all sorts of records had been knocked sideways when Chelsea beat Luxembourg's amateurs, Jeunesse Hautcharage, 21-0 on aggregate, Osgood helping himself to eight of the goals.

But it was a fatal eight-day period at the end of February and beginning of March which was to have even greater repercussions.

Orient won an FA Cup-tie 3-2, coming back from two goals in arrears. Worse, the following Saturday, Stoke City, very much the underdogs on this occasion, scored a late goal in the League Cup Final at Wembley, hitting for six the thought of a trio of major Cup wins in successive seasons.

Suddenly the 'Kings of Stamford Bridge' were villains rather than heroes, and barracking, virtually unheard for a decade or so, shattered the belief and confidence of many within the club.

In the autumn of 1972, Bill Garner arrived days after his heading ability had proved a thorn in the flesh for Chelsea's defence in a League Cup-tie at Southend. Otherwise, the cast was virtually un-changed, although several appeared to have lost much

Chelsea defending against Liverpool at Stamford Bridge in March 1972. The game ended goalless.

of their previous sparkle, the appetite for success not what it had been.

A final place of 12th was Chelsea's lowest in the First Division since promotion ten years earlier. And while there were days, in Cup football at any rate, when the old flair and determination seemed to be returning, it was never sustained.

Arsenal, deservedly won a sixth-round replay in the FA Cup at Highbury after a magnificent first con-test at The Bridge, which included a vintage goal from Peter Osgood, and some close shaves for the Gunners' defence which was a little fortunate to survive.

In the League Cup there was another semi-final. Along the way the highlights were two testing

Chelsea line up before the start of the 1972-73 season. Back row (left to right): Kember, Dempsey, Droy, Webb, Hudson. Middle row: Bonetti, Hinton, Osgood, Harris, Garland, Hutchinson, Mulligan, Phillips. Front row: Houseman, Cooke, Boyle, Baldwin, Hollins, McCreadie.

August 1972 and Chelsea internationals Peter Osgood and Eddie McCreadie look on as the young Wilkins brothers Ray (right) and Graham try out their ball skills.

John Hollins MBE
– Non-stop Dynamo

Apart from one brief interval, John Hollins was part of the Stamford Bridge scene for a quarter of a century. Born in Guildford, he first walked in through the Stamford Bridge gates as a fresh-faced boy of 15 to join Chelsea's youth scheme in 1961. From that moment his progression to professional status, on his 17th birthday, and to first-team player one month later, was as inevitable as it was natural.

For 12 years he was Chelsea's midfield dynamo, covering literally thousands of miles in his number-four shirt, spraying passes to his front men with minute accuracy and frequently joining in the fun himself, making solo bursts which often resulted in an explosive strike on goal.

He was, in short, the complete midfield player, his ability to win the ball from physically more powerful opponents deceptively betrayed by his lightly-built frame. It was difficult to find any time in a game when John was relaxed, or stationary. And all the while his high-pitched vocal encouragings could be heard as easily by his fans on the terraces as by playing colleagues on the park. Almost 600 appearances and more than 60 goals – a marvellous return for a nominal signing on fee.

Only once, against Spain in 1967, did he gain full international recognition, but he was one of a clutch of his contemporaries who won three major Cup-winners' medals for Chelsea. Twice the fans voted him their 'Player of the Year'.

The Chelsea of Hollins' first 12-year spell at The Bridge thrived on success and, indeed, was expected to win trophies. Alongside his great talent and flair was a superb attitude towards the game. Some of his more mercurial colleagues might be prone to fluctuations of form and lack of commitment at times. But John rarely allowed his own standards to dip. Off-days were rare. He was self-motivated, his temperament ideal, whatever the occasion. Anything less than 100 per cent effort totally unacceptable.

But, there was darkness as well as sunshine in his Chelsea times. In 1975, in common with several others of those triumphant Cup sides, he was allowed to leave just at the very time he should have been leading the Blues through their difficult period of transition. One generation was fading, its successor needed the leadership and inspiration John could have provided.

After both Queen's Park Rangers and Arsenal profited from his abundant qualities, John returned to Chelsea after eight years away, as manager John Neal's player-coach. From 18th position in Division Two the previous season, and with Hollins now at 'number two', Chelsea won the championship of that division, the youthful enthusiast of earlier years now a staid and highly-respected professor, preaching as well as practising.

Chairman Ken Bates on re-signing John already recognised him as 'our next manager'. And, 12 months later in June 1985, he succeeded Neal, perhaps, with the knowledge of hindsight, a year or two too soon. For 12 months all seemed well. Chelsea were progressing along the right course. Then, as with Sexton 20 years before, cracks first appeared and then widened.

Man-management is a delicate operation at the best of times, and now personalities clashed. Discontent and rumour became rife as results on the field deteriorated alarmingly. Morale plummeted throughout the club and, amid mounting speculation, Hollins was sacked.

That such a distinguished and likeable man should end his Chelsea days in this manner was one of the saddest episodes in the club's history. He walked away bitterly hurt and disillusioned by the experience and feeling let down by those unable to match his own standards.

Right: Ron Harris appears to be up-ending QPR's Stan Bowles at Stamford Bridge in February 1974.

Left: Alan Hudson and Colin Harvey of Everton at Stamford Bridge in December 1972. The game ended 1-1, watched by over 23,000 fans. Right: August 1973. Manager Dave Sexton and Ron Harris leaving an FA disciplinary hearing which looked into allegations that Harris appeared in a game against the British Police XI whilst under suspension.

struggles with champions Derby County, a dour defensive display at the Baseball Ground being a prelude to a closely-fought replay in which the Blues' defence was sorely tried in the closing stages, precariously holding on to a 3-2 lead.

The real drama, however, was reserved for the semi-final. After an anaemic display in the first leg at home, when Norwich City scored two early goals before successfully boarding up their own goal against prolonged bombardment with some good defensive work, the Canaries were 5-2 ahead on aggregate in the second instalment, with six minutes remaining. Whereupon, without prior warning, a tidal wave of fog, coming from the river end at Carrow Road, totally obliterated the proceedings. After a 25-minute wait, the referee made one brief abortive attempt to re-start the game, but was left with no option but to abandon the match.

Even so, Chelsea were unable to take advantage of their reprieve, and lost the third match by a single goal in this remarkable tie watched by over 100,000 spectators.

When the 1973-74 season began it was quickly apparent that, for the second time in eight years, there were fingers on the self-destruct button.

From the outset form, and results, were indifferent. The hard core of the Cup-winning teams were still available, apart from McCreadie and Weller. Gary

Locke had secured the right-back position for himself and Micky Droy had taken over Dempsey's centre-half berth. Several other newcomers, too, started to make their mark, among them Ian Britton, John Sparrow, Ray Wilkins and Kenny Swain. But most of the problems were away from the pitch itself.

Matters came to a head on New Year's Day when Dave Sexton omitted four senior players from the side, against Sheffield United at Bramall Lane. Within days Alan Hudson had signed for Stoke City, for a new record British transfer-fee of around £240,000. Two months later, Peter Osgood had also departed, to Southampton, and, immediately after the end of the season, David Webb moved out too, joining Queens Park Rangers.

For the time being, at least, the directors backed Sexton in his surgical operations. But, not least for the fans, it was heart-breaking to see the most successful side in Chelsea's history needlessly disintegrating. A final position of 17th in the League, and exits from both Cups at the first hurdle, summed up a situation which should never have been allowed to develop. Stubborn intransigence and lack of man-management skills had destroyed what had been so patiently created.

And overseeing it all was the forbidding outlines of the new giant East Stand, repeatedly delayed and months behind schedule. Ominously, severe financial problems, too, were now rearing their ugly head.

Seven Years And Seven Managers

CARLISLE United were the unlikely visitors to Stamford Bridge on the opening day of the 1974-75 season. "It is the beginning of a new era in the history of Chelsea Football Club, marked by the opening of our magnificent East Stand," boasted Brian Mears. After the Cumbrian side had purloined two points, in their first-ever fixture in this division, some 30,000 supporters were left to ponder on what other surprises this new promised land had in store.

If things on the field were scarcely meriting the attention of the sports headline writers, those speculating on what was happening behind the scenes certainly were eye-catching. And, on 3 October, after much rumour, David Sexton resigned his post as manager.

In many ways his departure was similar to that of Docherty in 1967. The two most successful managers in Chelsea's history had been unable to keep the ship on course once they encountered rough water. In Sexton's case it was his failure of man-management and, as soon as his previously faithful disciples turned on him, there could be no compromise between the parties. No halfway meeting point, with both prepared only to speak but not listen.

There was no new appointment from outside. Assistant

Ray Clemence dives to take the ball from Chelsea's Ian Hutchinson at Stamford Bridge in August 1974. Chelsea lost 3-0 and at the end of the season were relegated.

manager Ron Suart took over in a 'caretaker' capacity and then, after five weeks, was given full control, with the assistance of Eddie McCreadie as coach.

From the outset the main objective in an already serious situation was to avoid relegation. Five games in December, with seven points out of ten, suggested the corner could be turned, but the closing nine weeks, bringing a mere five points from nine matches virtually sealed the team's fate. Even so, as late as the middle of April hope flickered briefly, until a two-goal defeat against Tottenham at White Hart Lane settled

Chelsea's new manager Eddie McCreadie looks pensive as he watches his side in action against Tottenham Hotspur at White Hart Lane in April 1975 with the Blues teetering on the brink of relegation. Spurs won 2-0 and Chelsea's fate was almost sealed.

Chelsea at the start of the 1975-76 season, back in Division Two. Back row (left to right): Dempsey, Droy, Richardson, Sherwood, Garner, Hutchinson. Middle row: Harris, Hinton, Stanley, Swain, Locke, Sparrow, Langley, Maybank. Front row: Britton, Cooke, Graham Wilkins, Ray Wilkins, Finnieston, Bason, Wicks.

Steve Wicks and Peter Bonetti are helpless as Paul Mariner scores for Plymouth against Chelsea at Home Park in September 1976 but the visitors went on to win 3-2.

Ugly scene during the League Cup fourth-round tie at Highbury in October 1976. Chelsea lost 2-1, but at the end of the season they were back in Division One.

Chelsea boss Eddie McCreadie wonders just what is happening as spectators invade the pitch when Chelsea beat Hull 4-0 on the last day of the 1976-77 season. Chelsea had already assured themselves of promotion seven days earlier.

matters. On the eve of this important confrontation Ray Wilkins was handed the captaincy of the team, at the age of 18 the youngest player in the club's history to be given this honour.

By now, with Chelsea's future in mind, McCreadie had been appointed team manager, Suart 'moving upstairs' as general manager.

Before this 1974-75 season had begun, a club record fee of £225,000 had obtained the services of David Hay, a Scottish international midfield player

from Celtic, who had been one of the outstanding players in the 1974 World Cup. Otherwise, the only newcomer was John Sissons, an outside-left from Norwich City who had previously spent most of his career at West Ham. Unfortunately, Hay was immediately handicapped by a series of personal misfortunes and was rarely to fulfil his potential in England. Stalwarts from happier days remained, among them, Hollins, Cooke, Ron Harris, Houseman and Kember. Bonetti had been superseded in goal, for the time being, by John Phillips and Hutchinson, emerging temporarily from long periods on the treatment table, was leading goalscorer.

But it was a makeshift outfit at best, and the remedy for Chelsea's problems could not be immediate, more especially in view of the alarming escalating financial crisis.

The escape route from the Second Division was never likely to be quick or easy. McCreadie's enthusiasm was transferred to his charges and, had the impressive home form been reflected by similar success on foreign soil, Chelsea would have been running with the leaders. And indeed, nine points from a possible ten in the month of November suggested a serious challenge for promotion could be expected, but thereafter things turned sour.

Ian Hutchinson's prolonged struggle with injury ended in defeat, and early retirement, at the age of 28. He had been an integral part of Chelsea's best times. More happily, Peter Bonetti, ludicrously pensioned off the previous summer, was recalled after a brief sabbatical in North American football. Defeat at Crewe in

Chelsea at the start of 1977-78. Standing (left to right): Hay, Locke, Finnieston, Wicks, Droy, Garner, Dempsey, Langley, Sparrow. Seated: Phillips, Graham Wilkins, Lewington, Walker, Harris, Stanley, Bonetti. On ground: Ray Wilkins.

the Football League Cup was an undignified exit in that competition but after promising more in the FA Cup, Crystal Palace won a tense fifth-round tie, by the odd goal in five, after Droy had been taken away with a broken elbow, in front of more than 54,000 customers at Stamford Bridge. Despite that, home League attendances fell to their lowest level for 52 years.

In the autumn of 1976, the club was forced to call in a firm of leading accountants, as a result of which debts of £3.4 million were revealed as creditors unanimously agreed to a one-year moratorium. Economies included vacating the training ground at Mitcham, while for the second season in succession, no transfer fee was paid for playing reinforcements, urgently needed though they were. Rather, eyes turned towards the juniors who again were producing a stream of talent of high potential. Among this latest batch were Steve Wicks, Graham Wilkins, Teddy Maybank, Steve Finnieston and Tommy Langley.

Against this unpromising background, McCreadie

Three members of the Wilkins family on the eve of the 1977-78 season. From left to right are Graham, Steve and Ray.

worked wonders. An excellent start to the season restored morale and self-belief. By the end of September, Chelsea were leading the field, and the crowds were returning, expecting to be entertained, and were seldom disappointed. Finnieston and Kenny Swain, with 40 goals between them, proved a powerful attacking combination. Behind them 'Butch' Wilkins, now an English international, Ian Britton, and newcomer Garry Stanley beavered away industriously in front of a defence, more solid than for several seasons. Hay, injury-free, at least for the time

Micky Droy and Steve Wicks are bisected by Aston Villa's John Deehan at Stamford Bridge in November 1977. Less than 20,000 fans saw a goalless draw.

Boxing Day 1977 and David O'Leary lashes hammers home Arsenal's third goal against Chelsea at Highbury. Peter Bonetti is grounded and the rest of the Chelsea defence in disarray.

being, had his best season in a blue shirt and Bonetti cheated the passing of the years with some vintage goalkeeping performances.

Taking over the leadership at the end of September, Chelsea held this position for more than six months, until Wolves, main rivals throughout most of the winter, nosed ahead on Good Friday as the teams entered the final straight. A 4-0 defeat at the hands of Charlton Athletic proved an isolated hiccup before a

New manager Ken Shellito poses for the cameras after taking over at Stamford Bridge in July 1977.

Ray Wilkins – An Old Head on Young Shoulders

WHEN the latest clutch of Chelsea Juniors assembled for school in the autumn term of 1971, Raymond Colin Wilkins was head boy. Not only did he stand out from his colleagues in terms of ability on the football field, but also as regards qualities of leadership. His brother, Graham, an altogether different character, had passed through the school 12 months before.

Almost immediately Ray, or as his father himself a former professional with Brentford, nicknamed him, 'Butch', was given his first-team debut in October 1973. Tasting the atmosphere of senior football, he was allowed two substitute appearances, with a more extended trial following in April.

For Chelsea, it was a time of transition. The 1970 and 1971 sides were falling apart. Manager Sexton, allowing matters to slip from his control was also soon to leave, and the general atmosphere at Stamford Bridge was scarcely conducive to introducing a promising newcomer.

By the time the 1974-75 season was under way a bad situation had deteriorated still further. Ron Suart, briefly, and Eddie McCreadie, Sexton's successors, were vainly attempting to rescue a ship, fast sinking into a lower division, without any cash available for repair work.

It was at the beginning of December that 'Butch's' first-team career began in earnest. At the age of 18, he was being asked to succeed Alan Hudson in his role in midfield. Unlike Hudson he was surrounded by teammates floundering in a sea of uncertainty, their confidence shaken by events off the field, as well as the notable lack of success on the playing area.

However, rather than accept the inevitable, Wilkins sent to work by example, his talents rising above the mediocrity of some of those around him; his enthusiasm fired by McCreadie's own drive and constant encouragement. Matters came to a head on 19 April with three fixtures remaining, the first, and key, game against Tottenham at White Hart Lane. Leading Chelsea on to the field that afternoon as the club's youngest-ever captain, even Ray Wilkins was unable to prevent an inevitable defeat, and relegation which duly followed seven days later.

For another five seasons he wore the skipper's armband with distinction, always leading his men from the front. For two of those years he was never once absent from his post. In 1976-77 his troops were rewarded with promotion back into the top division; two years later, with McCreadie now in American football, it was relegation once again.

In this comparatively brief period, and against the odds, 'Butch' had managed to establish his place in the England team, his 24 full caps overtaking Woodley's previous Chelsea record.

His qualities were abundant. Usually operating in front of the back-four defensive wall, his passing was immaculate, both in its range and accuracy. At times he was criticised for his lack of ambition. For playing 'safe balls' rather than going for the pass which splits open the enemies' defences. Maybe, at one stage of his career, this was a fair judgement, but it proved merely a temporary phase. Another asset was his shooting skills. From around the edge of the opponent's penalty area he was always prepared to pepper the target and often to catch the goalkeeper unawares.

He left Chelsea, both to further his own career, and to help to solve the club's financial problems, the £825,000 fee for his transfer to Manchester United easily a club record up to that time.

After Manchester, it was Milan, Paris and Glasgow. Then back to England in November 1989, most improbably on a free transfer. Many at Chelsea felt that it was sad that he chose Queen's Park Rangers rather than allowing the wheel to turn its full circle. Up to the end of the 1996-97 season Wilkins was still playing in the lower divisions and 'Butch' is held in the greatest respect, and admiration, by those who recall the lad with the long hairstyle starting out on his road to the top from The Bridge in the 1970s.

David Stride (extreme right) knees away a corner against QPR at Loftus Road in November 1978 with Peter Eastoe, Ron Harris and Stan Bowles amongst the watching group.

crucial point, chiselled out from a vital confrontation against the leaders at Wolverhampton on the penultimate Saturday of the season, ensured promotion, leaving Hull City's visit, seven days later, to be an occasion for celebration, a crowd of 43,000 revelling in a 4-0 victory for the Blues.

There were signs, too, that under the careful stewardship of Martin Spencer, Chelsea's financial guru, monetary matters were gradually being brought under control. But not before another bombshell exploded. During the summer Eddie McCreadie had been unable to agree personal terms for a new contract and had resigned, a crippling blow and one which should surely have been avoided with a measure of common sense and give-and-take.

His contribution in his two seasons in charge was remarkable. He had made big strides in rebuilding the club's playing resources without resort to a cheque book. Morale had been restored and the jovial atmosphere of the earlier days of Docherty and Sexton recaptured. His departure to American football was a loss not only to Chelsea, but to the British game as a whole. Hurriedly, his old full-back partner Ken Shellito was promoted from his position as youth manager. Certainly after 22 years at The Bridge he knew the place inside out. But coaching the younger players was his forte, and keeping Chelsea afloat in the

top class in what was to be his only full season as manager was itself no mean feat.

David Hay was missing for virtually the entire 1977-78 season. Four old stagers, Bonetti, Ron Harris, Droy and Locke, lent stability to the defence. Ray Wilkins was outstanding in midfield, while Langley chased and chivvied tirelessly in attack, aided by Swain and Finnieston, along with Clive Walker a new recruit whose days of brilliant opportunism could unfortunately by no means always be relied upon.

A win against Manchester United at Old Trafford and a glorious 4-2 FA Cup victory over the reigning European champions, Liverpool, were notable events, and a final 16th place was no mean achievement in such difficult circumstances.

There was to be no such consolation 12 months later. Never at any time during the nine long months of the 1978-79 season did it seem remotely likely that Chelsea could avoid another relegation experience. One bad result followed another with depressing regularity and when Shellito resigned in December the position was once again one of desperation.

By appointing the legendary Danny Blanchflower, the famous Irish international and captain of the Spurs 'double' side, as his successor, the directors took a gamble. Since his playing career ended in 1963 he had been out of the game and working as a sports

Aston Villa's Alan Evans scores a disputed goal at Stamford Bridge in December 1978. It gave Villa victory and Chelsea plenty to worry about.

journalist. He simply loved football. He was a theorist who would expound his ideas to many an enthralled audience who might, or might not, be able to follow his reasoning. Certainly his players at Chelsea never responded to his rhetoric, or fully understood where he was trying to take them.

Players moved out. Some like Bill Garner were pensioned off, others brought in cash to fill up the empty coffers, among them Steve Wicks and Kenny Swain who threw in their lot with Derby County and Aston Villa respectively.

Blanchflower's recruits included Duncan McKenzie, a mercurial figure and brilliant artist with the ball, and Eamonn Bannon a Scottish half-back from Heart of Midlothian who, sadly, never settled into the English game. And with Bonetti's 21-year Chelsea career finally over, his successor was the Yugoslav 'keeper Petar Borota. Brilliant one day, awful the next. Never consistent, he loved to entertain the crowd with his unique brand of showmanship and clowning. The Chelsea fans took him to their hearts, prepared to overlook his blunders and frequent disasters. Meanwhile, Chelsea managed a mere five League victories and their total of 20 points was a new, and unwanted club 'record'.

Early in the following season, after ten months in charge on a month-to-month contract, Blanchflower resigned. Ever an idealist, he was simply the wrong manager at the wrong time in Chelsea's history and, sadly, he had lost touch with much of the reality of the modern game during his years out of soccer. It was an unworthy end for one of the finest men football has known.

Weeks before his departure, Blanchflower had appointed one of England's 1966 World Cup heroes, Geoff Hurst, as his coach and right-hand man and within six weeks the former West Ham man had been given the post of manager on a permanent basis, with Bobby Gould as his deputy. This time Brian Mears was more guarded in his welcome but rightly pointed out, "Because of the managerial changes we have experienced in the last two or three years it is essential we bring an air of stability to Stamford Bridge."

When Blanchflower left in the middle of September, Chelsea occupied 18th position in the Second Division, the lowest placing in their history. The metamorphosis was immediate and spectacular. Five consecutive victories catapulted the club into fourth spot in the table with confidence soaring. The only two newcomers of note were John Bumstead, setting out on his long and honourable Chelsea career as a midfield player, and Mike Fillery, with his obvious creative skills, potentially a star of the future.

With a three-point lead and standing five points clear of the fourth club, the Easter festival was approached with high hopes, but, all at once, the team, which had picked themselves up to perform so well under Hurst and Gould, tumbled at the final hurdle. After Oldham Athletic had been defeated, 3-0, in the final fixture, hundreds of excited fans charged across the ground, singing and dancing, as the team appeared at the front of the directors' box. Chelsea, their programme completed, were now one point ahead of Sunderland, and occupying the vital third place in the table.

However, the Wearside team still had one fixture to fulfil nine days later, against West Ham United, when Chelsea joy turned to disappointment as Sunderland duly won the game, leaving the Blues out in the cold, on goal-difference. Nevertheless, even that bitter blow could not disguise the fact that under, their new management team, it had been a remarkable renaissance.

Equally positive was the early part of the 1980-81 season. Only one defeat in three months, from September to the beginning of December, was a continuation of the previous year's form. A five-point lead

December 1978 and another new Chelsea manager, Danny Blanchflower, meets groundsman Harry Cassells.

Chelsea's newly-signed Yugoslavian goalkeeper Petar Borota dives at the feet of Kenny Dalglish in the goalless draw at Stamford Bridge in March 1979. John Sitton is the Chelsea defender on the right.

Chelsea salute their long suffering fans after the last home game of 1978-79, a 1-1 draw with Arsenal. They drew 1-1 at Old Trafford two days later and were back in the Second Division.

Chelsea boss Geoff Hurst and his assistant Bobby Gould with the club's newly-painted badge before the start of the 1980-81 season.

at the head of the table seemed to emphasise that Chelsea were storming their way to promotion.

Often playing with two wingers, Peter Rhoades-Brown, Clive Walker, or Phil Driver, and with Colin Lee, a £200,000 recruit from Tottenham Hotspur, leading the forward line the goals came readily enough, six of them against Newcastle United at The Bridge. Dennis Rofe, from Leicester City, provided experience and stability in a defence in which Gary Chivers was now playing alongside Micky Droy.

Suddenly, it all went horribly wrong, and even Chelsea had never experienced quite such a dramatic about-turn throughout their 75 years. First, came a six-match sequence without a victory. Swiftly, that was followed by nine games in which not a single goal was scored, a spell involving 848 minutes playing time.

As a consequence, Chelsea plummeted to below halfway in the table to occupy their lowest-ever position, and, for the third year in succession, failed to survive one round in either of the Cup competitions.

In April, Geoff Hurst and Bobby Gould, now villains rather than heroes, were sacked with 18 months of their contracts still to run. Hurst later abandoned a proposed High Court hearing for wrongful dismissal, after Chelsea had agreed to settle matters with 'substantial compensation'.

Immediately the board appointed John Neal as the club's new manager. Not since Ted Drake, almost 30 years before, had the club sought an incumbent with such managerial experience. After six occupants of the chair in seven years, it was a welcome change of policy. Neal, a quiet, shrewd man from the North-East had already performed creditably at Wrexham and Middlesbrough and was tough enough to meet the greatest challenge of his career.

However, before he could get to grips with the situation, an even greater change had occurred. Brian Mears had not only resigned the chairmanship of the club, after 23 years on the board, but he was not even remaining as a director.

He had grown up with Chelsea, from his schooldays as part of his family's dynasty. As a boy he had seen the team win the League championship, before, the 'Prince of The Bridge', as Danny Blanchflower once described him, he savoured the Cup triumphs of 1970 and 1971.

He made mistakes, of course, notably with the timing of the building of the new East Stand, which was too long delayed. He was, at times, indecisive, and tended to seek too many opinions. But, at the last, he was subjected to unfair pressures, not least from the fans, whose hostile judgments could not take into account the full facts of the case. In the end this amiable and likeable man bowed to mounting pressure and responded, acting as he always had, 'by doing the decent thing'.

Without doubt, he left Stamford Bridge in a world much different from that in which his great-uncle, Gus began the Chelsea story, 77 years before.

John Neal – Too Briefly And Ken Bates Arrive On Stage

IT DID not take John Neal, with his assistant manager, Ian McNeill, long to discover the enormity of the task he had been given. At once, almost in deference to tradition, it seemed, Chelsea began to reproduce performances defying all belief and forecasting. One week the faithful army of away supporters suffered the ignominy of seeing Rotherham United, in the Second Division basement at the time, plant six goals past Borota at Millmoor without reply, then to be followed seven days later by a highly creditable 2-1 victory against Newcastle United. As a result of such unpredictability, it was to be a season of mid-table anonymity so far as the League campaign was concerned.

With home attendances in 1981-82 dropping to their lowest in Chelsea's history, at least the faithful fans had some compensation in the FA Cup. Replays were needed to eliminate both Hull City and Wrexham, unpromising overtures for the visit of mighty Liverpool to Stamford Bridge in the fifth round. Now, however, the Blues chose the big occasion to answer their many critics, and the pundits, who universally had expected the inevitable.

From the moment Peter Rhoades-Brown opened

John Neal, appointed Chelsea's new manager after Hurst and Gould were sacked with 18 months of their contract still to run. Neal soon realised just how big a task he faced.

the scoring with a deadly left-foot drive, the European champions were reeling and, when Bruce Grobbelaar could do no more than palm away Clive Walker's accurate cross for Colin Lee to volley the loose ball into the net, a famous victory was assured.

Next on the list were Tottenham Hotspur, with Chelsea again being drawn first out of the hat for the fourth time in succession. When Mike Fillery drove a free kick past Ray Clemence, as his defenders continued their argument with the referee, another shock result seemed to be on the cards.

But three goals in 14 minutes, the result of a spell of magic football from Spurs, killed off such fancies, Alan Mayes replying late on to give the score-sheet a look of respectability which Chelsea's efforts deserved.

Again, with finances still as tight as ever, Mr Neal had little chance to remedy weaknesses. At least Colin Pates had now emerged to bolster the defence, with Lee often as his central partner, once Droy had been forced out of action with injury. Chris Hutchings, from Harrow Borough, was another inexpensive recruit for the back division.

Far more important than such trivia was an event off the field, which was to have far-reaching consequences. In April, Kenneth Bates, a former chairman of Oldham Athletic, purchased Chelsea Football Club and provided the lifeline so desperately needed. Succeeding Viscount Chelsea as chairman almost immediately, he changed the traditional image of the club and began what was to prove to be a Herculean task by putting the club on a professional business basis and clearing out much of the dead wood which had been allowed to accumulate over the years.

Problems, and not least that of Chelsea's escalating minority hooligan element, were tackled head-on. Everyone, from first-team players to tea-ladies had to justify themselves, or be shown the door. Efficiency, rather than sentimentality, became the order of the day, and, in the dire circumstances prevailing, were necessary steps if the club was to survive. The practical help of supporters, too, was enlisted.

During the summer of 1982 there had been a few changes on the professional staff also. Peter Borota had moved out, to be replaced in goal by the more dependable, and promising, Steve Francis, while Ian Britton, Graham Wilkins and Dennis Rofe had also left. Two newcomers, of contrasting ilk, were veteran 'Pop' Robson, at the age of 36, also to help the coaching staff, and the little known David Speedie, from Darlington, a wonderful investment at £80,000, and the first of several excellent purchases by manager John Neal. His operating of the transfer market was one of his greatest strengths.

Neal clearly expected immediate success. "We've got to be prepared to provide exciting and attacking football – as well as go for promotion. I think, with everyone pulling in the right direction and giving all they've got, we have a very good chance of achieving that goal", was his pre-season assessment of the situation. In fact, Chelsea failed not only to fulfil those hopes but experienced comfortably the worst season in their entire history and ended up in 17th place in the Second Division table.

At one stage, even that ignominious position looked out of reach. Saturday, 7 May 1983 proved to be one of the most crucial days in Chelsea's history. On an afternoon of weather more usually experienced in the depths of winter, the team travelled to Lancashire for a match against Bolton Wanderers which was to decide which of the two famous clubs would be relegated, a sombre meeting which took place in front of a miserable gathering of 8,687 spectators.

So dreadful was the fare provided that a goal, at either end, seemed most unlikely. Whereupon Clive Walker produced that special brand of opportunism which was very much his trademark. From 25 yards range he unleashed a shot, swerving wickedly in the wind, which sped into the top corner of the net to decide the issue. Seven days later, a goalless draw in the final fixture was sufficient to steer the club into safe water, still only two points clear of the relegation trio, among them Bolton Wanderers.

Ken Bates had described Chelsea as a "sleeping giant, a stately home run down" adding "with care, patience and enthusiasm we can be back in the First Division – where we belong". A drastic situation was met with a drastic remedy. Before the curtain went up on the 1983-84 season, nine players with first-team experience, among them the wayward Mike Fillery, Gary Chivers, Alan Mayes and 'Pop' Robson had been shown the door. Into their places came seven newcomers, six of whom were to underline John Neal's gifts in working the transfer market on a shoestring budget.

For less than £500,000, nearly half of which was recouped through incoming fees in any case, the manager had virtually built a new team. Eddie Niedzwiecki was a goalkeeper who at once realised his great potential. A commanding figure whose career was destined to be cruelly cut short by injury at the age of 28, by which time his prowess had already been recognised by the Welsh selectors. Scottish centre-half Joe McLaughlin proved a worthy and natural successor to Micky Droy, at any rate in the short-term. Nigel Spackman, plucked from Third Division Bournemouth, made the transition to the higher grade of football with immediate ease, and forwards Kerry

The most important goal in Chelsea's history? Clive Walker hits his spectacular winner against Bolton Wanderers at Burnden Park in May 1983 and Chelsea are almost safe from relegation to the Third Division. Seven days later a goalless draw against Middlesbrough at Stamford Bridge ensured that the Blues would remain in Division Two - and 12 months later they were promoted back to the top flight.

Ken Bates, took over as Chelsea chairman and soon made a dramatic impression on an ailing club.

Kerry Dixon heads home Pat Nevin's cross at Blundell Park in May 1984 and the celebrations can begin as Chelsea clinch the old Second Division title. It was Dixon's 28th goal of the season.

Colin Lee was a fine striker when he came to Chelsea but the advent of Speedie and Dixon limited his chances and he developed into a full-back who played a major role in the latter part of the 1983-84 promotion season.

Dixon and Pat Nevin embarked on new careers which, rapidly made them household names.

Two former pupils made up the septet. John Hollins returned as player-coach and Alan Hudson, at 33 and back from North American football, was given a chance to revive his career and also assist the younger players, a gamble which, most unfortunately, was lost through injury.

"I've never bought so many players in such a short space of time", said Neal. "But they have to be blended into the right formation. We must achieve this as quickly as we can."

Ninety minutes after the start of the 1983-84 season, a shell-shocked, much-fancied Derby County were wearily dragging themselves off the Stamford Bridge pitch having helplessly watched five goals rifle into their net. From that launching pad Chelsea's promotion campaign took off, momentum rarely faltering. Only one defeat, against Sheffield Wednesday at Hillsborough, from the first 17 games set the tone. And a battle royal for the leadership, with Wednesday, became the feature of the season. From the beginning of December, Chelsea were never below second place in the table. With three matches to go, the Yorkshire team were five points ahead, the championship seemingly their's, both teams already assured of promotion.

The championship prize, however, was the one Chelsea had set their hearts on, and a storming finish enabled them to pip Wednesday on the post, on goal-difference. The final fixture, at Grimsby with nearly 10,000 Chelsea fans present, triggered off wild celebrations as Dixon's goal, his 28th of the season, clinched a famous victory – and the Second Division title.

Not only had Chelsea been successful, their accomplishment had been achieved with style. The supporters had been richly entertained with positive, non-stop, attacking football. Dixon and David Speedie formed an irresistible attacking force down the centre. Pat Nevin's artistry exposed many a defence before setting up goalscoring gifts, this apart from scoring 14 times himself. His skills, indeed, bore comparison with many names of Chelsea's past, and continued the club's tradition of putting fine entertainers before their public.

David Speedie celebrates a goal with Kerry Dixon. Speedie and Dixon formed a superb attacking combination down the middle.

Behind them, Niedzwiecki's firm handling and reliability never faltered in goal, and McLaughlin and Colin Pates established a happy and formidable pairing in central defence with Hollins, now at right-back, an important influence early on. Once more, at least on the field, Chelsea could look forward with confident expectation.

Obviously, a sterner examination lay ahead, but no season since the dizzy days of Docherty and Sexton began with expectation so high as that in the autumn of 1984. After a somewhat stuttering beginning, there were few alarms. From mid-October onwards the team maintained a comfortable position in the top half of the table.

Not for 12 seasons had Chelsea made a significant mark in knock-out football and now, anxious to right this omission, they seized the chance in the League (now Milk) Cup. Millwall, (who were to extract revenge in the FA Cup), Walsall, and Manchester City were overcome, in turn, in the first three rounds of the competition, before Sheffield Wednesday, especially anxious to put the record straight after the drawn-out rivalry of the year before, were quarter-final stage opponents. A 1-1 draw at Stamford Bridge proved a mere cocktail what was to follow at Hillsborough in one of the most memorable ties in Chelsea history. By half-time and losing by three clear goals, that match, to all intents and purposes, seemed over.

The substitution of Paul Canoville at the interval, in place of Colin Lee, seemed of little significance, until, sprinting like a greyhound out of the traps, the newcomer announced his arrival by scoring within 11

seconds of the restart. Twenty minutes later, the gap was further narrowed when Kerry Dixon beat Wednesday's 'keeper in a 'one-against-one' confrontation, so that when Mickey Thomas grabbed an equaliser,

Pat Nevin's artistry combined with Speedie and Dixon to expose many First Division defences in 1984-85.

Kerry Dixon
– The Kerrygold Scorer

IN HIS SHORT (many would say too short) time at Chelsea, manager John Neal operated the transfer market with great skill, his working knowledge of latent talent, especially in the lower divisions of the Football League, proving invaluable.

Pride of place among his list of successful acquisitions must go to Kerry Dixon. At £165,000, his signing from Third Division Reading ranks as one of the best investments ever made by Chelsea Football Club. Other big clubs, well aware of the big man's potential, hesitated, whereas Neal pounced.

Goalscoring was always in Kerry's blood. His father, in a brief career with Luton Town and Coventry City, managed a dozen goals from less than a score of games, before he drifted into the non-League game in order to pursue his other, and more remunerative, occupation.

Kerry's route to the top of the tree was never easy or straight-forward. He was a part-time player with Tottenham Hotspur during the 1978-79 season but failed to make the grade. Spells at Chesham United and Dunstable followed, before he was rescued from comparative obscurity by Reading where his career blossomed. 56 League goals from 116 League games, many scored with great panache, alerted several clubs to his potential.

Two goals in his Chelsea debut, against Derby County at Stamford Bridge on the opening day of the 1983-84 season, immediately won over fans who, increasingly, were to take him to their hearts in the years ahead. He was, in partnership with David Speedie, a crucial element in winning the Second Division championship that season.

Some critics were quick to point out shortcomings in both technique and skills and were reluctant to regard him as genuine international material. Yet, the fact remains that his four goals for England from eight outings (three of them after being summoned from the substitutes bench) is a ratio not lightly to be dismissed.

Kerry was ideally built for a striker, a natural athlete. At 6ft in height, and weighing around 13st, he could take care of himself and withstand physical challenge. He was a fine header of the ball, and as is the case with the best of his breed, could climb above the ball to direct it downwards with power and accuracy. On the ground his first touch could sometimes leave a little to be desired, but his speed and powerful finishing were major compensations for a certain lack of finesse.

For three seasons the goals simply flowed. Then, in January 1986, an injury, sustained in an FA Cup-tie, against Liverpool, kept him out of action for a month and many felt that he was never again quite the same player, his goalscoring not as prolific as hitherto, as his pace and acceleration appeared less devastating. Or maybe he needed a new challenge?

Ultimately this came after Southampton had paid £575,000 for his services in July 1992. At The Dell, he again, briefly, renewed his partnership with Speedie. But the change of environment did not suit him and further injuries prevented his new employers from getting value for money.

Written off by many, his career was later rescued when Luton Town, in desperate financial straits, took a chance by signing him, first on loan, in the early months of 1993. Again, often an absentee on the treatment table, and now almost aged 32, he rose to the challenge. Adapting his game to the limitations imposed by the passing of the years, he became provider rather than executor, his experience and great tactical awareness proving most valuable assets to his younger colleagues. First he was a vital factor in steering the Hatters clear of the (new) First Division relegation zone, before helping to guide them to an FA Cup semi-final where, appropriately Luton's opponents were …Chelsea.

Only Bobby Tambling stands above him in the Blues' all-time list of goalscorers and although he had set his heart on overtaking him, this was not to be. However, in ten happy years at The Bridge he had proved almost as popular as anyone throughout the Chelsea story, always being assured of a kindly welcome on his return, and totally immune from the modern and regrettable treatment of insult and derision which crowds now often reserve for their former heroes.

David Speedie heads Chelsea's winner at Stoke in May 1985. Mickey Thomas (11) and Joe McLaughlin are the other Chelsea players. Despite a 2-1 home defeat by Norwich City in the final game of the season, Chelsea finished a creditable sixth in Division One, yet only two years earlier they had faced relegation to the Third Division for the first time in the club's history.

Canoville's second goal, to make the score 4-3, almost seemed part of the script of this remarkable game. With Hillsborough rapidly emptying, as disgruntled and disbelieving home supporters started for home, a late and ill-judged tackle by Doug Rougvie inside the penalty area presented Wednesday with their lifeline. The final act of a remarkable evening saw Chelsea win the toss for the right to stage the third instalment which, perhaps not surprisingly in view of earlier events, the Blues won 2-1.

Sunderland, at that time waging a battle to stay in the First Division, which was to end in failure, seemed a reasonable semi-final hurdle to surmount. But ill-luck in the first 'leg' at Roker Park saw the home team emerge with a vital two-goal advantage, thanks to two penalties awarded against the unfortunate Dale Jasper, the second hotly disputed. At The Bridge an early goal from Speedie suggested all might be well. But two typical goals from Clive Walker, now wearing a red and white shirt in front of his former fans, irretrievably settled the tie.

Nevertheless, a final position of sixth in the First Division was highly encouraging, a UEFA place being narrowly, and agonisingly, missed thanks to defeat in the final home fixture.

Neal had added strength to his squad. Joey Jones, already a hero with The Shed, was an enthusiastic and ubiquitous defender. Darren Wood, who never established a happy relationship with the fans, and Scottish international Doug Rougvie also strengthened the rearguard. Mickey Thomas, unpredictable both on and off the field, was a great asset in midfield, with his bottomless supply of energy, and Gordon Davies provided excellent cover for Dixon and Speedie.

It seemed as if the mixture was right for further progress, and yet by the time new season dawned changes had been made. John Neal had been moved upstairs to the boardroom. John Hollins was appointed manager in his place, and Ernie Walley had arrived from Crystal Palace as first-team coach. Opinions were divided on the implications of the changes. But for the time being, at any rate, attention was more focussed on such problems as the ever-present hooligan minority which attached itself to the club and, of course, the future of Stamford Bridge, still in the melting pot. That this was so was due not least to the extraordinary action of David Mears, who had seen fit to sell his sizable share-holding in Stamford Bridge Properties to Marler Estates, a firm of property speculators. A most appalling and regrettable conclusion to his family's 80-year connection with Chelsea, and something which could well have destroyed the Football Club.

'Doctor' Campbell Finds The Remedy

WHILE there were many who were surprised that the Chelsea board had seen fit to reorganise the management team during the summer of 1985, by removing John Neal from his post, there were few serious misgivings expressed at the time. Down the years there had been few more popular, or more respected, players than John Hollins, Neal's successor. He knew from long experience the strengths, and pitfalls, peculiar to Chelsea and seemed well-equipped to cope with the tribulations which affect all managers from time to time. Furthermore, none of his 13 predecessors in the manager's chair had taken over in more propitious circumstances, with such a strong and talented playing staff.

Major surgery was not required. Rather, the team needed another calm, guiding hand at the tiller. A man who could draw out the potential of some highly promising performers in order to satisfy the fans hunger for success.

His first season in charge did not produce startling progress, but Chelsea maintaining their sixth place in Division One was no mean achievement. And, although Liverpool ended Chelsea's FA Cup aspirations at the second hurdle, the team fought their way into the last eight of the League Cup before Queen's Park Rangers won their replay at Stamford Bridge, in extra time, after goalkeeper Eddie Niedzwiecki had been carried off with an injury.

At least Chelsea managed to forge their way back to Wembley after a 15-year interval in the newly-formed Full Members' Cup. Maybe it was a minor and largely irrelevant competition, but nevertheless one which still managed to attract almost 70,000 spectators to the stadium to see a gripping contest with Manchester City, ending 5-4 in Chelsea's favour, City ensuring a grandstand finish with three late goals to banish any complacency, and setting the nerve-ends jangling. Few, however, agreed with Ken Bates' post-match comment: "The match was so exciting it was almost a disappointment that City didn't get their fifth goal and take the game into extra-time."

Not surprisingly, there were few new faces on parade. Jerry Murphy, after ten seasons with Crystal Palace added strength, as well as creative ability, to the left side of midfield. Similarly, the skills of Micky Hazard, after several seasons in North London with Tottenham Hotspur, also strengthened this department.

Twelve months later the situation was far less happy. Just when the indications were that Chelsea were once more re-establishing themselves as one of England's leading football clubs, the team utterly

Above: Hat-trick hero David Speedie celebrates a goal in the thrilling 5-4 victory over Manchester City in the Full Members' Cup Final at Wembley in March 1986. Left: Two goal Colin Lee (left) and hat-trick scorer David Speedie with the Full Members' Cup after the win over Manchester City which produced nine goals.

failed to make an impression in any of the four senior competitions. The level of entertainment was miserly, as the team was constantly chopped about in an endeavour to produce some degree of cohesion and success, and home attendances slumped accordingly.

By the end of December, Chelsea were propping up the rest of the First Division table. A Boxing Day victory at Southampton, urgently needed, sparked off a revival so that by Easter at least all fears of relegation had been banished. Even so, only for a single week during the entire season had the team eased their way into the top half of the list.

No fewer than 29 players were called upon. Signings included the return of Steve Wicks, from Queen's Park Rangers, Gordon Durie, a young Scottish striker of great potential, and defender Steve Clarke, from St Mirren, who was to give stability to a fragile defence over the seasons to come.

More worrying was the number of senior players moving out, their usefulness to the club, one would have thought, by no means exhausted; Nigel Spackman (to Liverpool), David Speedie (Coventry City), Doug Rougvie (Brighton & Hove Albion) and the gifted, if mercurial, Paul Canoville (Reading) represented a considerable weakening of the playing resources. Clearly the 1986-87 season witnessed a notable step in the wrong direction, but, much more seriously, was merely a foretaste of what was to follow.

At least by the time the troops had reassembled for Hollins' third campaign the cheque book had been produced to paper over some of the cracks. Tony Dorigo, a positive and aggressive full-back, had arrived from Aston Villa. The Wilsons, Clive and Kevin from Manchester City and Ipswich Town respectively. And Roger Freestone, a young, promising, Welsh goalkeeper who, almost at once, was to succeed the unfortunate Niedzwiecki whose all-too-brief playing career was about to terminate on the operating table at a time when he was mounting a take-over bid for the Welsh goalkeeper's jersey.

The prospects again seemed bright. "There is certainly a buzz of excitement around The Bridge as we prepare for the big kick-off", said Hollins. "I'm really optimistic about our chances this season."

What followed was one of the most disappointing of Chelsea's 72 campaigns up to that time. Dressing-room discontent surfaced almost immediately, and the team, third in the table by the end of September, went into a decline unprecedented in the club's history.

From the end of October to early April, the failure to win a single League game, in a sequence of 21 fixtures, established a new, and unwanted, record. Various tactical formations were tried without success. The team was utterly lacking in co-ordination, or with any settled system, and the lack of a dominating figure in midfield put intolerable pressure on an already suspect rearguard. Only Micky Hazard, with his consistently accurate passing ability in midfield, did not repeatedly give the ball away to grateful opponents.

In attack Kerry Dixon, now receiving the ball less

John Hollins, the former Chelsea star who was elevated to manager at Stamford Bridge and found himself with a strong playing staff.

frequently, lost confidence. Gordon Durie's finishing was wayward and unreliable (more than half of his dozen League goals coming from the penalty spot) and Kevin Wilson, with a higher scoring rate than anyone else, was often omitted in favour of, supposedly, striking weapons of higher potential.

Reading, themselves in a relegation season, and Swindon Town eliminated Chelsea from the League and Full Members' Cups, both opponents reducing the defence to tatters, and a visit to Old Trafford in the fourth round of the FA Cup proved equally abortive against powerful Manchester United.

On 22 March, with the situation now totally out of control, John Hollins and Chelsea parted company following weeks of newspaper speculation, much of it uninformed and wide of the mark. A month earlier, first-team coach, Ernie Walley, also departed, unloved, his exit unlamented by the players.

Hollins' situation was different. "I am genuinely sorry John has left," wrote Ken Bates. Inevitable though it was, it was sad indeed to see one of Chelsea's most distinguished servants walk away, disillusioned and distressed at events. Like others before him, this most likeable man had discovered that coaching and football management are poles apart.

Walley had already been replaced as first-team coach, without Hollins' blessing, by Bobby Campbell. Immediately after John's exit he was promoted to acting manager, his position being confirmed on a permanent basis before the end of the season.

Bobby Campbell, appointed first-team coach without Hollins' blessing, he eventually took over as manager when Hollins was sacked.

Campbell, with managerial experience, having been in charge at Fulham and Portsmouth, and also having held coaching assignments at Queen's Park Rangers and Arsenal, was, however, never likely to be a long-term appointment.

Mathematically, it was possible for Chelsea to steer clear of automatic relegation and, indeed, had Charlton Athletic not obtained a decidedly fortunate equalising goal in the final League fixture, the team would have squirmed out of trouble after Campbell's arrival had produced one win and five draws from eight fixtures.

The 1986-87 season had seen the introduction of the Play-off knock-out system to decide the final promotion and relegation place in each division. As a result Chelsea were given an 11th-hour lifeline to salvage something from the wreckage of their disastrous experiences.

A 2-0 victory against Blackburn Rovers at Ewood Park was confirmed by a 4-1 margin in the second leg of the semi-final to set up a confrontation with Middlesbrough, only recently rescued from oblivion after the Official Receiver had locked the Ayresome Park gates, with the club apparently on the verge of folding completely.

The first instalment of this final chapter gave the Teesside club a two-goal advantage after a hard-fought encounter in the North-East. Durie's early goal in the second match quickly raised hopes, but the Middlesbrough defence, exhibiting impressive poise and covering, held out under pressure to nail down the escape hatch.

In truth, taking Chelsea's performances over the previous nine months, they scarcely deserved any reprieve. What they also did not deserve were the appalling scenes of crowd violence which occurred at the conclusion of the Middlesbrough match, and which caused the Stamford Bridge terraces to be closed, by order of the Football Association, for the first six fixtures in the following season. A sad postscript to an even sadder season.

At a time when Chelsea's seven-year tenure of the Stamford Bridge stadium was coming to its end, the financial implications of relegation were especially serious. With Marler Estates suggesting a £40 million price for Chelsea to buy the freehold, a 'Save the Bridge' appeal had been launched. Chairman Ken Bates, meanwhile, determined not to be outwitted, or to accept defeat, was drawing up his own battle lines.

But, by the time Blackburn Rovers appeared again at The Bridge in August 1988, it was back to business on the field with the obvious target of returning to the First Division in the shortest possible time, and with only the vast expanses of empty terracing a depressing reminder of the events of three months earlier.

Indeed, Bobby Campbell had already announced before the start of the season: "My immediate managerial aim is to restore Chelsea to their rightful place at the top – we are the Manchester United of the South." While few dispassionate observers would agree with such hyperbole, it at least revealed his resolve, a resolve which was underlined by the pre-season acquisitions of Graham Roberts and Peter Nicholas. Roberts' reputation as a 'hard man', after service with Tottenham Hotspur and Glasgow Rangers, was soon in evidence on the field, while Nicholas, also with experience of football in the capital, as well as north of the border, likewise injected steel into the midfield department. So much so, that the loss of skills through the departure of Pat Nevin and Roy Wegerle were scarcely felt. The talented Wegerle, in fact, had never succeeded in persuading his employers of his ability to conform, or fit into a tactical framework. More to be regretted was the loss of Steve Wicks, like Niedzwiecki, forced into retirement through injury.

After an unsteady start, promotion was rarely in doubt, the Second Division championship ultimately being won by a margin of 17 points. Along the route all sorts of club records fell by the wayside. Never before had Chelsea won so many games (29) or chalked up so many points (99). Nor had the 27 League games without defeat between October and April previously even been approached. This sequence had also included Chelsea's record victory on foreign soil, 7-0 at Walsall.

In attack the Dixon-Durie attacking duo proved too hot for most Second Division defenders to handle. Together they shared 42 goals between them, a total that would have been still higher but for a series of illegal challenges on them inside the 'box', some of which helped Roberts to reap a rich harvest of another 12 goals from the penalty spot. Dixon, particularly, recovered his former zest and enthusiasm. Kevin McAllister, too, filling the gap left by Nevin, fully justified his elevation to the first team.

Only once during the season did Bobby Campbell feel obliged to enter the transfer market. In January he paid £725,000 for Dave Beasant, the need for an experienced goalkeeper to succeed Niedzwiecki having been apparent for some time.

In the shortest possible time, therefore, the damage of 12 months earlier had been repaired. If the euphoria was noticeably less than in the Second Division championship season of five years before, it was partly as a result of the strong feeling that such a salvage operation should never have been necessary in the first place. The average home attendance figure, less than 16,000 for League games, was significant, and by no means entirely explained by the enforced closing of the terraces at the start of the season.

Above: Nevin, Durie and Clarke are happy because Durie has just scored in the 1988 Play-off Final second leg against Middlesbrough at Stamford Bridge. But after extra-time it was 'Boro who emerged triumphant 2-1 on aggregate and Chelsea were doomed to Second Division football once more.

Left: Gordon Durie, whose partnership with Kerry Dixon yielded 42 goals between them as Chelsea returned to the First Division as champions of the Second. Durie scored five goals at Walsall in February 1989 as Chelsea recorded their biggest-ever away victory.

Right: Tony Dorigo, signed from Aston Villa. He made a great impression in the 1988-89 Second Division championship campaign and the following year won his first full England cap.

At Least A Stadium In Which To Perform

BOBBY Campbell occupied the manager's chair for another two seasons. Having put the patient back on its feet, the first of these campaigns consolidated Chelsea's place in the First Division. In fact, only two indifferent spells, in December and at the beginning of February, prevented the mounting of a serious assault on the championship. In any case finishing fifth in the table was eminently satisfactory.

There were few changes in personnel. Alan Dickens, the only signing of note before the season began, struggled to find his form and disappeared altogether after losing his place through injury before Christmas. A more important acquisition was the Norwegian international, Erland Johnsen, who took over Roberts' role in central defence to strike up a successful partnership with Ken Monkou, born in Surinam but recruited from Dutch football. In front of Beasant, in goal, and flanked by Clarke and Dorigo, Chelsea's defence was tighter than for several seasons. With Gordon Durie, again injury-prone, Kevin Wil-

son once more proved an able replacement, scoring 14 goals from the 34 in partnership with Kerry Dixon.

In the Cup competitions, ignominious defeats, at Scarborough in the League Cup and against Bristol City in the FA Cup, were balanced by the second success in four seasons in the Full Members' competition, still ignored and shunned by several of the top clubs. It was, nevertheless, a useful source of income for all that, with more than 76,000 flocking to Wembley to see Tony Dorigo's South American style free-kick win an otherwise dreary Final, against Middlesbrough, a partial revenge for the defeat in the Play-off Final of two years earlier.

With a sound basis on which to build, high hopes were once more expressed about the prospects for 1990-91. Moreover, still perilous though Chelsea's financial position was, Bobby Campbell was allowed to shell out more than £2 million for the signings of Andy Townsend, the Republic of Ireland's generalissimo, and Dennis Wise, a key component in Wimbledon's escalation to becoming one of the country's

Middlesbrough goalkeeper Stephen Pears can do nothing to prevent Tony Dorigo's 'South American style' free-kick which settled an otherwise dreary Zenith Data Systems Cup Final against Middlesbrough at Wembley in March 1990.

The victors pose for the cameras after they beat Middlesbrough to lift the Zenith Data Systems Cup. Back row (left to right): Beasant, Johnsen, Kevin Wilson, Bumstead, Dixon, Lee. Front row: Monkou, Nicholas, Hall, McAllister, Dorigo, Durie.

top football clubs. Balancing these two notable additions to the staff, only Clive Wilson, who had never fully lived up to his potential at Stamford Bridge, and Micky Hazard, on his day an outstanding dictator of play, had left.

Yet, apart from progressing to the semi-final stage of the Football League

Kerry Dixon scores Chelsea's second goal in the Rumbelows Cup quarter-final against Tottenham at White Hart Lane in January 1991. Chelsea went out to Sheffield Wednesday in the semi-final.

(Rumbelows) Cup, the season never properly took off. Hovering below the halfway mark for the first four months, five consecutive victories, including one at Old Trafford against Manchester United and another in a ten-goal extravaganza in the Midlands against Derby County, took the side into the top six in the list, as it turned out for the only time. Once more, a case of promise proving greater than fulfilment.

Also, as so often in the past, Chelsea seemed better equipped when it came to knock-out football, even though home defeats at the hands of Oxford United and Luton Town (after a penalty competition in the FA and Full Members' Cups) were humiliating experiences.

In the League Cup, Walsall (by a 9-1 margin on

aggregate), Portsmouth (after a thrilling replay at Fratton Park) and Oxford United (this time) were eliminated in turn, before the fifth-round draw produced a confrontation with Tottenham Hotspur, so often rivals in this sudden death type football down the years. A goalless draw at Stamford Bridge was disappointing, but White Hart Lane proved an inspiration, as Chelsea cantered home with goals from Townsend, Dixon and Wise, from the penalty spot.

Far different was the semi-final story. Maybe, finding themselves up against Second Division opposition bred complacency? Whatever the reason, a listless performance at Stamford Bridge in the first leg gave Sheffield Wednesday the priceless cushion of a two-goal advantage, a margin of victory which they

Dennis Wise scores from the penalty spot against Spurs. Chelsea dumped their North London rivals out of the Rumbelows Cup with a memorable 3-0 win.

Chelsea and, as John Hollins had done in a similar role three years before, had then created a favourable impression. But he had completely failed to make any mark whatsoever in his brief time, and his first managerial post, at Reading. The fact that he was by no means Chelsea's first choice, too, scarcely suggested it was a wholly confident decision, or one to boost his ego.

repeated at Hillsborough. As depressing as the result itself, and its implications, was the apparent total lack of commitment and determination against a team noticeably exhibiting those very same qualities.

Increasingly, it became clear that Campbell's days were numbered and even before the season ended it was announced that he was stepping down, to be replaced by the Scotsman, Ian Porterfield, forever remembered for his FA Cup-winning goal for Sunderland, at Wembley in 1973.

Not for the first time Chelsea found themselves at a crossroad. In some ways the choice of the manager seemed curious. From August 1988 to November 1989, he had been Bobby Campbell's assistant at

On the credit side, at least he knew the strengths, and minefields, at The Bridge. "We have a good squad and don't need an awful lot to be a successful side," he said on his appointment.

What followed was an all too familiar scenario of inconsistency and under-achievement. Frequent activity in the transfer market bore mixed fruit. Paul Elliott, at £1.4 million, a dominating central defender with experience of British and Italian football, was Chelsea's second most expensive purchase. Tommy Boyd, a Scottish international defender from Motherwell, never settled into the picture and returned north of the border after a few months. Football's legendary hard man, Vinnie Jones, certainly tough-

Dennis Wise rams the ball home in the 3-3 draw against Luton Town at Stamford Bridge in April 1991.

Kerry Dixon scores one of his two goals in the 2-2 draw at Goodison Park in April 1991.

In the penultimate game of the 1990-91 season, Chelsea scored an impressive 4-2 win over Liverpool at Stamford Bridge with Dixon, seen here scoring, again netting twice.

Chelsea's Kenny Monkou gets the better of Oldham's Graeme Sharpe at Boundary Park in August 1991.

Hull City, on Humberside, Everton and Sheffield United at The Bridge, were dispatched in turn without a goal being conceded and a third consecutive home draw, against Second Division Sunderland then in the process of disentangling themselves from relegation problems, did not seem an insurmountable obstacle. However, a positive first-half display, with Allen giving Chelsea the lead, was not sustained after the interval and the Wearsiders' equaliser was by no means an unfair indication of the run of play.

The replay at Roker was an altogether more dramatic affair, brought to the boil when Dennis Wise equalised Sunderland's first-half goal, with five minutes remaining. But, it has often been said that a team is at its most vulnerable when it has just scored, and so it proved on this occasion. Lax defending at a corner-kick allowed Sunderland a 'free' header to win the game.

Porterfield, as he must have realised, did not have time on his side. Patience was wearing thin with the financial repercussions from the repeated lack of success growing ever greater. Further, the formation of the Premier League at the start of 1992-93 with its complex television cash tie-ups increased pressure on managers, already sufficiently haunted by fear of failure.

After the goal famine of the previous season big money had been paid out for three strikers by the time the new season began. Robert Fleck, even at the time, seemed an expensive purchase at £2.1 million. Mick Harford, past his 34th birthday, was inevitably a short-term asset. John Spencer, with a handful of first-team appearances at Glasgow Rangers and Morton, a speculative signing for the future. Otherwise, seasoned Irish international defender, Mal Donaghy, was the only other addition of note.

For four months the signs were encouraging. At Christmas Chelsea were proudly perched in fourth place in the League table, five points behind leaders Norwich City. In addition, they were still alive and kicking in the Football League Cup, one of the last eight teams in the competition. And if the goals were not exactly flowing, at least the defence was better organised and more solid than for several seasons. This, despite the tragic loss of Paul Elliott with a serious long-term knee injury picked up at Liverpool in September, and which ultimately terminated his career.

ened up the midfield areas, while Clive Allen, a bargain buy at £25,000, scored nine times in 22 starts in four months, before being shunted off to West Ham United. With Kerry Dixon's star now in decline it seemed a strange decision, as was the transfer of home-spun central defender, Jason Cundy, to Tottenham Hotspur. This last transfer provoked vigorous and outspoken protests from supporters, so disenchanted had they become with the direction in which the club was moving.

In the League, the team hovered around mid-table for most of the time, before six defeats in the last ten fixtures condemned the club to 14th place, a poor reflection of the playing quality at Porterfield's disposal.

In the Cup competitions there were mixed fortunes. In the League Cup, Chelsea fell at the first hurdle, after a petulant display at Tranmere. Another assault on the Full Members' Cup came to a halt in the Southern Section Final, Southampton, struggling in the League at the time, winning both legs as Chelsea seemed quite unable to summon the necessary spirit or enthusiasm for a not-too-difficult task. Only in the FA Cup were hopes raised.

January, however, saw optimism fly out of the window in a disastrous eight-day spell. Crystal Palace won a fifth-round League Cup-tie on a near-waterlogged surface at Selhurst Park. Then, after a home defeat in a League fixture, Middlesbrough proceeded to eliminate Chelsea from the FA Cup on a dark, miserable, evening on Teesside, scoring two goals in the last 20 minutes, after an own-goal had put the Blues into the lead.

Nigel Winterburn challenges Kerry Dixon at Highbury in October 1991.

As so often, that triggered a landslide. History repeated itself for the umpteenth time. Thirteen games without a win saw the team tumble below the halfway mark in the League table. The goals dried up, and, so alarming was the transformation, that even relegation was becoming an outside possibility. It came as no surprise, therefore, when the chairman acted decisively at the end of February.

Ian Porterfield was replaced by David Webb as Chelsea's manager. In admitting that he had reservations about the situation as long ago as the previous October, Ken Bates claimed he was aware that short-term success was merely papering over the cracks.

Even so, Webb's appointment, unusually, was merely 'for the rest of the season'. But he attacked the situation with all the verve and aggression he had exhibited as a player. "I know Chelsea and know what people respond to at this club," he announced on arrival. "I will live or die by my actions. Time will tell if I make the right ones".

Kevin Lock, the former West Ham and Fulham

Chelsea's Graham Stuart (far right) celebrates a goal at Hillsborough in August 1992.

Graham Stuart and Crystal Palace's Simon Rodger during the League (Coca-Cola) Cup quarter-final at waterlogged Selhurst Park in January 1993.

Andy Townsend and Dennis Wise and Manchester United's Mark Hughes at Old Trafford in April 1993.

player, joined the coaching staff, as the highly-respected Don Howe, a guru among coaches, moved out. The new regime certainly made an immediate impact.

Webb's first game in charge produced a defeat at Blackburn. "Not the sort of performance I expect from Chelsea. We must work harder and be more professional", was his reaction. A dozen more games remained and these produced five wins, as many as in the previous four months, and four draws, as against only three defeats. Immediately his teams conveyed a confidence and sense of purpose which, certainly in Porterfield's latter days, had been totally missing.

In his final message to supporters, at the beginning of May, Webb was able to say: "I am pleased with the way things have gone. The goals I set out when I arrived have largely been achieved". And with a prophetic foreboding about his future at the club he added: "Whether I am involved or not at the start of next season, I sincerely wish the very best for the club and supporters". And on 4 June, as Webb may have guessed, Glen Hoddle became Chelsea's 12th manager in 20 years.

It had been an unsettled switchback of a season. Some 32 players had made first-team appearances. While injuries added considerably to selection difficulties, Porterfield never seemed sure of his best side, which understandably served to breed confusion and lack of confidence.

Of the newcomers only Donaghy and, up to the time of his departure to Sunderland in March, Harford, justified their transfer fees. Nigel Spackman returned, after five years away from the fold, but dropped out through injury almost at once. Beasant's increasing fallibility in goal prompted the recall of the more predictable Kevin Hitchcock, and, later, the purchase of Dmitri Kharine from the CIS (the former Soviet Union). But a clutch of former juniors were also making their presence felt, among them Graham Stuart, shortly to move to Everton, Eddie Newton, Frank Sinclair, Andy Myers, Darren Barnard and Craig Burley. Billy Birrell's legacy, from nearly half a century before, lived on.

Probably more significant, and of more permanent impact, however, was the purchase of Stamford Bridge Stadium by The Royal Bank of Scotland in December 1992. This deal, highly favourable to Chelsea FC, at long last opened the way for the development of the ground into an envisaged 40,000 all-seater arena. Years of negotiations, and set-backs, had ended in a victory as important as any in the Chelsea story. A rich and lasting reward, indeed, for chairman Ken Bates' indomitable persistence and tactical astuteness in debate and endless legal wrangling.

Hoddle's Passing Gospel

GLENN HODDLE had already tasted life at Stamford Bridge. In 1991 he spent six months with Chelsea after leaving AS Monaco, on a free transfer, recovering from an injury which had threatened

to terminate his playing career. So successful was this rehabilitation that not only was he able to resume his place, as player-manager, on the field, but for two highly successful seasons at Swindon Town he showed that he had lost none of his priceless skills on the ball and, indeed, little in the way of pace. Furthermore, his tactical awareness was as sharp as ever.

Having piloted Swindon into the Premiership, for the first time in that club's history, not surprisingly, his move to take over Chelsea caused some acrimony in Wiltshire. But, as he said, "I am delighted to be working with a big club. In the months I did spend here a couple of years ago it was an eye-opener for me. I am very much aware the fans are craving for success."

With Peter Shreeves as his 'number two,' and with Graham Rix in charge

Chelsea celebrate a good start to the 1993-94 season with the Makita Trophy.

Gavin Peacock scores against Sheffield Wednesday in the fourth round of the 1993-94 FA Cup. It was sweet revenge for the Owls' victory in the 1991 League (Rumbelows) Cup semi-final. This time it was Chelsea who were on the way to Wembley.

Chelsea players celebrate Peacock's goal against Manchester United in March 1994 at Old Trafford. It proved the winner and earlier in the season the same player had given Chelsea another 1-0 win over the seemingly invincible Premiership champions.

of the juniors, he made an immediate impact. Not for Hoddle the direct 'long-ball' route to goal, humping the ball forward in the vague hope that, sooner or later such unattractive tactics will produce something positive.

From the opening fixture of the 1993-94 season, a home match with Blackburn Rovers (lost 2-1), the new 'passing-game' style was immediately recognisable, as was the need for patience. For most of the players, it involved a re-education in their approach to the game. Hoddle's gospel was being superimposed on men brought up to other ways, and whom he might, or might not, have selected to put his principles into practice on the field.

Single-goal victories over Manchester United and Liverpool, in September, suggested that the transition period would not be prolonged or too painful. But then

Peacock is on the mark again and this time Dennis Wise offers congratulations after the striker's goals against Luton Town in the 1994 FA Cup semi-final at Wembley.

Steve Clarke — They Also Serve

It was a combination of Chelsea's efficient scouting system north of the border, patience, and Ken Bates' friendship with the St Mirren chairman which brought Steve Clarke to Chelsea for a bargain £420,000 in January 1987. One of the club's most loyal servants had arrived.

Seldom hogging the

limelight, Steve, born in Ayrshire, calmly accepted and lived with the ups and downs typical of so many who have served Chelsea for any lengthy period down the years.

His loyalty, efficiency and willingness to serve wherever needed in varying defensive formations,

have endeared him to Chelsea supporters for over a decade. And not the least of his assets is his seeming immunity from those vagaries of form which have afflicted so many others in the blue shirt.

Dependability is his trademark, and all this after an inhospitable introduction to the club on a bitterly cold and snowy day in the depth of winter at a damp Portakabin on Chelsea's training ground.

As a full-back, on right or left, sweeper, or in the centre of defence, Steve has quietly adapted his game to the wishes and whims of the seven managers under whom he has served.

Brave, strong, hard-working, deceptively quick – especially when going forward – he is an excellent passer of the ball, his accurate crosses and unselfish running into space have created innumerable opportunities for teammates down the years.

Over 400 senior appearances for Chelsea spread over 12 seasons is an impressive statistic. Yet he has experienced more than his fair share of injuries, including a double-hernia and a cartilage problem. Extraordinarily, too, one manager saw fit to relegate him into reserve team football for almost a year and he even found himself on the transfer list for a spell. Why then did he stay at The Bridge? "Because no one else ever wanted to buy me," was his smiling reply!

Despite it all, six full Scottish international caps have come his way, yet lesser performers have been more frequently recognised.

As the club's PFA representative 'Clarkey' is held in great respect. Bigger names, and more flamboyant players, may have attracted more headlines. More tellingly are such tributes which come from those inside Chelsea Football Club: "The perfect professional ... a pleasure to work with ... the kind of player every coach needs."

No one was more deserving of the three Cup-winners' medals which came his way in 1997 and 1998.

Chelsea skipper Dennis Wise and Manchester United captain Steve Bruce before the 1994 FA Cup Final.

things started to go awry. Dennis Wise, appointed captain by the new manager, was sent off at West Ham, his typically hot-headed reaction to an infringement leaving the referee with no alternative but to dismiss him. Form nose-dived. Manchester City, at Maine Road, provided a somewhat insipid third-round League Cup-tie which was lost, 1-0. And, following the win over Liverpool, 11 League fixtures passed without a victory, yielding a mere two points. Only Swindon Town, ironically, kept Chelsea off the bottom of the table.

Confidence evaporated, but Hoddle's belief in what he was trying to do never for one moment failed him. And a single-goal win against Newcastle United at The Bridge on 28 December proved the turning point.

By now the manager had spent over £3 million by bringing in Gavin Peacock from Newcastle, Danish defender, Jacob Kjeldbjerg, and Mark Stein, Stoke City's lightweight attacker, to bolster his squad. All three proved wise investments at any rate in the medium-term.

From the beginning, Peacock fitted naturally into a 'diamond' formation in midfield. Operating in the 'hole' behind the front strikers, Stein and John Spencer, and with Craig Burley (relishing his promotion into senior football) and Wise on the flanks, Eddie Newton completed the pattern by operating immediately in front of the zonal back-four. Earlier, Chelsea had experimented with a sweeper system, in continental fashion, which clearly was ill-suited to players, who struggled to come to terms with such a foreign idea.

The transformation in the New Year was remarkable.

In four months, the team moved from 21st place to 12th. And, after an unsteady beginning in the FA Cup, with Barnet, carrying the worst record in the League, almost snatching victory in their third round 'home' tie, switched from Underhill to Stamford Bridge for crowd safety reasons, the feeling that this could be 'Chelsea's Cup year' gathered momentum.

That sentiment was heightened by a splendid night's work against Sheffield Wednesday at Hillsborough, in a replay after a 1-1 draw at The Bridge 11 days earlier. As the manager said, "Our desire, mobility and closing-down were excellent." A glorious six-passing movement set up Spencer to give Chelsea an early lead. And, although a Wednesday equaliser forced extra-time, Peacock and Burley settled matters with goals, each of which was again the climax of intricate pattern-weaving.

Wolverhampton Wanderers proved dour opponents in the next round, at Stamford Bridge, but Peacock's opportunism won the day, as he scored the only goal of the afternoon. And it was again the same player who won the semi-final at Wembley, against Luton Town, with another brace of goals.

Twenty-four hours later, it looked as if Oldham Athletic would be Chelsea's opponents in the Final, until Manchester United obtained an equalising goal in the time added on for injuries, then going on to win the subsequent replay comfortably.

Injuries complicated Chelsea's preparation for their first FA Cup Final for 24 years. Hoddle had managed only two 'starts' since November. Stein had been missing

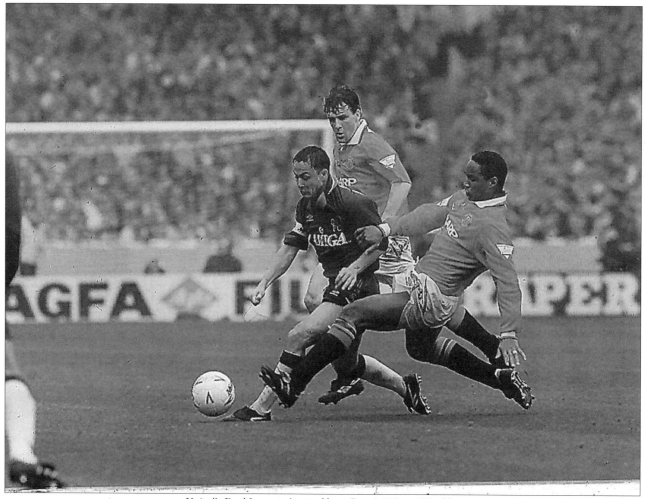

United's Paul Ince gets in a tackle on Dennis Wise at Wembley.

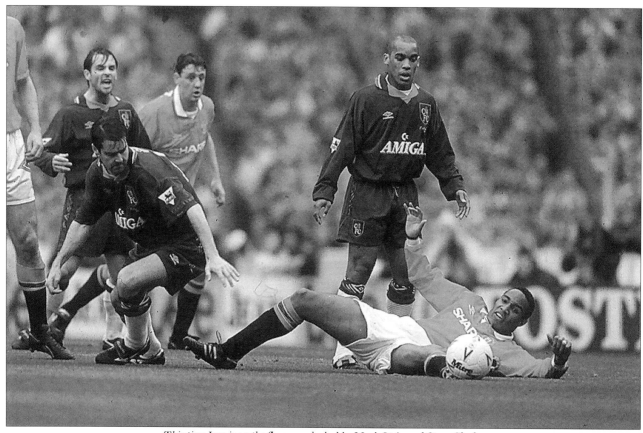

This time Ince is on the floor, overlooked by Mark Stein and Steve Clarke.

for 14 games before returning for the last League fixture, and scoring twice. Burley, too had suffered hamstring problems.

Manchester United arrived at Wembley, having already clinched the League championship, and therefore seeking to become the fourth team in recent years to achieve 'the double'. For 45 minutes Chelsea more than held their own. Peacock hit the crossbar and Frank Sinclair, Stein and Spencer all had shots scrambled away with a total lack of dignity and composure on United's part. Not once had the opposition managed a shot on target.

But all that was to change. A rash tackle by Newton, in the penalty area, produced the inevitable, spot-kick which put United into the lead, an advantage which was doubled five minutes later when Sinclair was also penalised in the area, this time harshly and in somewhat controversial circumstances. Immediately, Hoddle produced himself from the substitutes' bench, but only to watch helplessly as United went on to make it 4-0, and to rub salt into Chelsea's wounded pride, as well as giving the score-sheet a totally unrealistic appearance.

At least Chelsea were back in Europe, if only by virtue of Manchester United's qualification for the Champions' Cup leaving a gap for the Blues to fill in the Cup-winners' Cup.

And, not surprisingly after an interval of 23 years, it was the European scene which dominated the 1994-95 season, despite the manager's ambitious aims also to achieve success in the three major domestic competitions.

After an encouraging start in the Premiership, Chelsea had effectively lost touch with the leading group of clubs by the beginning of November, as well as being dismissed from the League Cup by West Ham United at Upton Park. The ultimate position of 11th in the table was a poor reflection of the ability and depth of the squad.

Even more disappointingly, Millwall won their fourth-round FA Cup replay at Stamford Bridge courtesy of a penalty 'shoot-out' after Stein had given Chelsea the lead 20 minutes from the end of normal time. But this setback was further aggravated by a crowd disturbance at the end of the game, involving scraps between rival supporters which were typically exaggerated by the media after the small minority had been efficiently dealt with by police and stewards. Chelsea Football Club were subsequently exonerated by a Football Association disciplinary hearing.

In order to meet the demands of a season, with the possibility of some 60 fixtures to fulfil, Hoddle had bolstered the three main departments of his squad by the signings of Scott Minto, a left-side defender, the England international midfielder, David Rocastle, and Paul Furlong, who had been a regular goalscorer with Watford.

For different reasons none of them made the impact expected, and only Minto was later to justify the manager's judgement and financial outlay.

However, disappointments on the domestic front were in large measure compensated by the exciting, and by no means unsuccessful, invasion of Europe, despite the irritating handicap, from Chelsea's point of view, of the rule limiting selection to three 'foreigners' and two 'assimilated' players. In effect this involved selecting any five from 11 such branded performers on the professional staff, and even produced the re-emergence of Graham Rix on to the battlefield, making his debut as a Chelsea player at the ripe old age of 36 years and 336 days.

Czechoslovakia's Viktoria Zizkov, first-round opponents in the Cup-winners' Cup, provided excellent entertainment in a 4-2 first-leg victory at The Bridge, after Chelsea's early lead had been pulled back to 2-2 before half-time. Fortunately, no such alarms occurred two weeks later in the second chapter when Hoddle's canny '4-4-1-1' formation ensured a goalless draw.

Austria Memphis proved stiffer competitors in the next round, achieving their object by chiselling out another no-score draw which, happily, proved insufficient thanks to a brilliant individual goal by John Spencer, fit to rank alongside any in Chelsea's long history, in the return match.

Gathering a long ball well inside his own half of the field, and with none of the enemy between him and the Austrian goalkeeper, the diminutive Scot set out on his lonely 70-yard mission with a gaggle of opponents in desperate pursuit. Outstripping them all, he completed his journey with a delicate chip to defeat the despairing dive of the 'keeper. And, despite pressure in an intimidating atmosphere, this remarkable strike was sufficient to win the tie after Memphis subsequently equalised on the 'away-goal' rule. "Our best performance in my time at Chelsea", was Hoddle's verdict.

Four months later, and less dramatically, goals from Stein and Furlong overturned a single-goal reverse at the hands of Club Bruges KV – history repeating itself after almost a quarter of a century – in the quarter-final of the competition to set up a meeting with Real Zaragoza at the next stage.

Sadly, this proved too big a hurdle to surmount after the Spaniards ran up a three-goal lead in their Romerada Stadium. But not before what Glenn Hoddle labelled 'our finest performance of the season' had produced an exciting 3-1 victory in the second game at Stamford Bridge to end a European venture which had lived up to all its promise for a new generation of the club's supporters. Zaragoza's subsequent victory in the Final of the competition served merely to enhance Chelsea's reputation.

Nevertheless, when the curtain fell there was, once again, the feeling that neither potential nor expectation had properly been realised, especially bearing in mind that as late as 15 April, relegation from the Premiership was a possibility - a two-goal victory against Aston Villa thankfully concluding a sequence of 12 home League games without a win at The Bridge, a new and unwanted 'record'.

Considerably happier was the occasion of Arsenal's visit on the last day of the 1994-95 season when

Mark Hughes attempts an acrobatic overhead kick against Mark Crossley of Nottingham Forest in 1995-96.

Glenn Hoddle ended his long playing career with a wonderful display of his artistic skills to enthral everyone in a 30,000 audience.

Now Hoddle was able to concentrate solely on his role as manager, in certain respects what proved to be his last season at Chelsea was broadly similar to its predecessor, despite the strengthening of the playing staff with four notable additions.

Ruud Gullit, renowned and respected throughout the world of football with a string. of impressive honours at both national and club level, could even lay claim to being the most famous name of all to wear the Chelsea shirt. At the age of 33, whether as 'sweeper', controlling midfield, or in attack, he thrilled and entertained the crowds wherever he played.

Mark Hughes, a second world-class acquisition, one year junior to the Dutchman,with a similar line of honours with Wales and Manchester United, was also to prove an influential asset, as indeed did Dan Petrescu, the versatile Romanian right-sided international and, briefly, Terry Phelan, a lightning raider on the opposite flank who unfortunately proved to be regularly prone to injury.

Even so, yet again no serious challenge on the Premiership title was even remotely likely in 1995-96 as results continued to fluctuate between the brilliant and the utterly deflating. Middlesbrough, for instance, were contemptuously sent packing by five clear goals in a thrilling exhibition of open football at the beginning of February as Hoddle declared. "The standard is now set

and we must try to achieve that every game." Six days later, Chelsea meekly subsided to defeat at Coventry in the most insipid manner imaginable.

More realistically, Chelsea's style and mental approach again proved more attuned to 'knock-out' football, despite a shock dismissal in the League Cup at the hands of Stoke City in October.

Happily, the FA Cup competition produced better days, notably in the third-round replay at St James's Park against Newcastle United. Twice the Magpies took the lead; twice Chelsea equalised, on the second occasion thanks to Gullit's goal two minutes from normal time. Then, after an abortive 30-minute extra period, Chelsea won the 'penalty contest' 4-2, with Eddie Newton's spot-kick ending a night of almost unbearable tension and sharing the limelight with goalkeeper Kevin Hitchcock, whose crucial save of Newcastle's second kick ultimately proved decisive.

Wins over Queen's Park Rangers, Grimsby Town, also after a replay, and Wimbledon, again requiring a second chapter, propelled Chelsea to their third semi-final in successive years, this time against Manchester United at Villa Park, which, although ending in failure, produced a magnificent contest.

Chelsea were already missing Petrescu, through injury, and an unfortunate set of circumstance followed. After Gullit had scored with a header, first Steve Clarke and then Phelan were forced to retire from the fray through injury, before a tragic misplaced pass 'gave' United the winning goal.

Dennis Wise is left floundering by Manchester United's Eric Cantona in the 1996 FA Cup semi-final at Villa Park.

As the manager summed up: "Semi-finals are about winners – and we weren't the winners."

And so, once more, a season which promised much subsided into disappointment, even though there were compensations. Despite the outlay of enormous sums of money to entice world stars to the Fulham Road, a steady flow of home-spun young players were also becoming increasingly influential. In addition to such as Craig Burley, Eddie Newton and Frank

Sinclair, new names, too, notably Michael Duberry, a commanding presence in defence, were starting to press their claims.

But the season did not quite finish when the curtain fell on the final fixture on 5 May 1996. Almost immediately, Glenn Hoddle was appointed to the post of England coach, to be succeeded by none other than Ruud Gullit, at the head of a 12-strong management team.

Another Change At The Helm – But Three Major Cups In Twelve Months

S O, once more, optimism was very much the key note when Ruud Gullit's squad of players reported for duty in the latter part of the summer of 1996, and immediately, his intimate knowledge of the European game and its players was revealed.

From Italy came Gianluca Vialli (a free-transfer bargain) and Roberto Di Matteo (at £4.9 million setting a new club record transfer fee), the two of them having already accumulated more than 70 international caps and two club championship medals. Then, in November they were to be followed by Gianfranco Zola, whose impact was such that six months later he was being recognised as the Football Writers' Footballer of the Year.

Chelsea's John Spencer, Gavin Peacock and Paul Furlong (who joined First Division's Birmingham City) were all to depart in 1995, as Ruud Gullit made space for his expensive foreign arrivals. Here, Paul Furlong tussles with Napoli's Policano during the Makita Cup match at Highbury on the eve of the 1994–95 season.

Less heralded was the French defender, Frank Leboeuf, who lost little time in winning the popul-

arity of his new fans whose adulation was almost immediately translated into song, heard up and down the country wherever Chelsea played.

Clearly the competition for places, even in a squad of limited numbers and further reduced by the unfortunate retirement, through injury, of Jakob Kjeldbjerg, together with the subsequent departures of John Spencer and Gavin Peacock, both of whom could look back on some memorable and influential days at Chelsea, was going to be intense.

The start was highly promising. Four 'clean-sheets' from the first five games left Chelsea in third place in the Premiership with the chance of taking over the leadership when they visited Liverpool, at Anfield, on 21 September.

However, a spate of injuries, which was to afflict the club throughout the season, had already begun to weaken Gullit's hand and caused frequent choppings and changes in his tactical formations.

Dmitri Kharine's season had already ended, his cruciate ligament ruptured, and ably though his (four) deputies, including the Norwegian goalkeeper, Frode Grodas, performed on occasions, his absence was sorely felt throughout the campaign.

Gullit's planned reliance on the 'sweeper' system also became especially disrupted, both by injuries to himself, and also to David Lee who managed less than 90 minutes of League football during the season. And with Leboeuf also an absentee through injury and suspensions at times, his selections were frequently dictated from the physiotherapist's treatment room.

Of equal handicap was the absence of the promising Michael Duberry whose season, after an already late start, was ended in January as a result of a ruptured Achilles tendon. And Eddie Newton, a growing and vital ingredient in the 'withdrawn' midfield role, appeared in less than half of the fixtures.

Inevitably, this caused repercussions. Most notable of all, Vialli's place was insecure once it was determined that Zola's effectiveness was greatest when playing with, or just behind, the striking thrust of Mark Hughes, who had an outstanding season. Even though ending as Chelsea's leading goalscorer in League games, he increasingly became a forlorn and isolated figure, a mere spectator, on the substitutes' bench.

In the circumstances, being in contention for a UEFA competition place until the final League fixture reflected enormous credit on both manager and playing staff.

But, as many times in the past, the greatest achievements were to be gained from cup football,

Gianfranco Zola
Smiling Gnome from Sardinia

FROM the moment he trotted on to the pitch for his Stamford Bridge debut against Newcastle United in November 1996, Gianfranco Zola's personal appeal and charisma were instantly communicated to an expectant crowd.

There was no question of a trial probationary period once he arrived in England. Within minutes of being introduced to his new

team-mates on the training ground, his skill and talents not only shone forth like a beacon but also lifted those around him. And so it continued.

His apprenticeship had begun at Napoli. His tutor, whom he later succeeded, was Diego Maradona. From the Adriatic port he graduated to Parma, where he won a UEFA Cup winners' medal, 12 months after suffering the disappointment of losing to Arsenal in the European Cup-winners' Cup Final.

International caps have accompanied him along his travels as he has become an integral part of the Italian team.

Fifty years ago a Chelsea secretary, marooned in a dungeon inside the club offices during matches, insisted that he immediately knew when a hero of those days, Tommy Walker, received the ball by the crescendo and upwelling of sound from the fans high above him. Now, 'Franco produces an identical reaction.

Often he gains possession in confined space, in a cul-de-sac, the ball coming at an awkward angle, while attracting physically intimidating opponents like moths to a lamp; a difficult situation being transformed into one seemingly impossible. Yet, like Houdini before him he extricates himself from imprisonment, disengaging his marker with deceptive ease and happily proceeding on his way. The hallmark of the true master.

When granted room to weave his magic, he becomes both a provider of goals for others and a deadly finisher himself. A tally of 63 goals from 136 games for Parma, this against Italian defences, speaks for itself. His Chelsea scoring-ratio confirms the fact.

The award of any free-kick within 35 yards from goal sets the Chelsea crowd alight with anticipation. That was the range from which he dipped the ball over the embarrassed Everton goalkeeper, also aided by a defender on the goal-line, causing many in the Stamford Bridge crowd to dissolve into helpless laughter.

Two weeks later, he humiliated another respected and experienced West Ham United defender by beating him, first on the inside, then round the outside, before cutting back to repeat the dose a third time and then scoring with a shot of fearsome velocity.

Or again, this time against Manchester United, he initiated an attack with a 40-yard pass and was in position, three moves later, to turn inside two bemused defenders to score another memorable goal past a goalkeeper totally bewildered by such magic. Goal of the month. Or any month!

Yet, perhaps even that piece of sorcery was exceeded by his arrival on to the Stockholm stage on that balmy evening in May 1998. Within 22 seconds after being summoned from the substitutes' bench, and with Chelsea struggling to unlock the stubborn Stuttgart defence, his second touch on the ball rifled a shot of venomous power past an astonished goalkeeper to settle the contest with a flash of his own, copyright, brand of genius.

despite a somewhat humiliating defeat in the third round of Football League (Coca-Cola) Cup at Bolton on Wednesday 23 October. Disappointing though that was, this reverse was completely overshadowed, and put into perspective by, the death of Matthew Harding, the club's vice-chairman, together with the pilot and four fellow passengers who were killed in a helicopter crash in Cheshire on their way home from the game.

From September 1993 he had been closely and actively associated with Chelsea, most notably in providing the money to launch the building of the North Stand which now bears his name, and purchasing the freehold of the stadium from the Royal Bank of Scotland.

Despite his periodic and much publicised differences with Ken Bates, he remained closely involved with all the later stages of the ground development. His close connections with the fans (he just wanted to be 'one of the lads') made him a cult figure known and liked by thousands in the game who had never met him.

The floral tributes, from all over the country, which swamped the area inside the main entrance at Stamford Bridge following his death were proof of the esteem in which he was held. Equally, the silence observed before the following home game was a moving and unforgettable experience. Many, unashamedly, were in tears.

And if Matthew was never destined to see Chelsea win a major trophy, at least he lived to know that Chelsea will henceforth be performing in a magnificently reconstructed Stamford Bridge.

Long since gone are the afternoons when the closing stages of a game would be played out to the accompaniment of the doleful sound of greyhounds baying in their kennels behind the north terrace prior to their excursions later in the evening. No longer do white-coated GRA officials scurry to propel the track floodlights into position as the football crowds disappear into the winter gloom. And who now recalls the giant black totalisator board, or the lines of betting windows at the rear of 'the Shed'?

Since 1974, when the East Stand was opened, the rest of the decaying stadium largely lay fallow until the North (Matthew Harding) Stand was opened in November 1994. Now, its counterpart at the Fulham Road end, including a modern executive (Galleria) tier, was opened in August 1997. Beneath is a large underground car park.

Even more excitingly, the final pieces in the Bridge jig-saw will be placed into position with the construction of the new West Stand, once planning permission is received bringing the capacity of the stadium to some 44,000, and making the capacity of Stamford Bridge the largest of any club ground in London.

Nor is that all, the Chelsea Village development embraces a 3-star, 160 bedroom, hotel; three restaurants, an apartment block and a business centre amongst its other facilities. A three-floor megastore

and a new administrative building for Chelsea Football Club, making use of the latest technology, is a further bonus.

With the co-operation of the Hammersmith and Fulham Council, the club will now have a strong commercial base from which to operate. Not least, in March 1997, Chelsea Village was successfully floated on the Alternative Investment Market, becoming one of the first football clubs to launch a share issue.

By that time Chelsea were already four steps along the FA Cup route to Wembley.

If a third-round home FA Cup tie against West Bromwich Albion was a somewhat undemanding start to the journey, the draw for the next stage, bringing mighty Liverpool to The Bridge, was a formidable examination.

And when Chelsea retired to the dressing-room at half-time on that late January Sunday afternoon, they were licking their gaping wounds, already two goals in arrears. Only super-optimists would have kept their diaries free for the later rounds of the competition. Yet the second-half period which followed will always rank among the most thrilling and spectacular ever seen at the old stadium.

From the moment Mark Hughes, hitherto a surprising choice for the substitutes' bench, entered the ring like an angry bull waiting to attack his prey, Liverpool's earlier ascendancy and confidence evaporated.

Defensively, Chelsea reverted to a 'back-three'. Eddie Newton and Dennis Wise successfully performed a 'holding operation' in front of the rearguard, allowing Roberto Di Matteo to run free, creating confusion and goalscoring opportunities galore, for 'Luca Vialli, 'Franco Zola and, not least, Hughes. Within five minutes the 'Welsh Dragon' had scored himself before setting up Zola for the equaliser, the latter a 'Collector's piece' even by the little Sardinian wizard's standards.

Thereafter, the result was seldom in doubt, although the defensive trio, and Steve Clarke in particular, were entitled to claim their share of the honours. Vialli it was, however, whose double strike, a close range stab-in and a powerful header, set the seal on a victory which will never be forgotten by those fortunate enough to have been present. "This will be the match of this season's FA Cup competition," was one immediate and accurate assessment.

Next on the menu was Leicester City in their home in the Midlands, presenting a tougher hurdle than some anticipated, and keeping their own prospects alive, after Chelsea had set up a two-goal lead after 35 minutes, by scoring twice in reply and equalising, just before the end.

The replay, only settled deep into extra-time through Frank Leboeuf's penalty, will unfortunately forever be remembered for the controversial circumstances which led to that award. Was Erland Johnsen's storming solo charge into the the area ended illegally? Or was he toppled by his own sheer momentum? That Chelsea were fortunate to win the referee's

Mark Hughes scores a superb goal in the semi-final against Wimbledon.

Erland Johnsen gets in a tackle on Wimbledon's Efan Ekoku in the FA Cup semi-final.

decision was an almost unanimous verdict. But then, Leicester had been similarly favoured by the award of the free-kick which produced their late equaliser ten days earlier.

First Division Portsmouth, at Fratton Park, turned out to be an altogether easier hurdle in the quarter-final, the 4-1 margin of victory being achieved with considerable style and panache. A bigger threat to Chelsea's progress, in fact, was the sea mist drifting over the ground from the nearby Solent and at one time threatening postponement.

The semi-final against Wimbledon at Highbury also proved a lesser examination than many expected. Perhaps the Dons were wearied by a congested fixture

list? But Mark Hughes, once more, stumped up with two goals as he and his team-mates showed no misplaced sympathy for a plea of exhaustion in a convincing 3-0 victory.

And so to the biggest occasion of all. Maybe the opposition, Middlesbrough, could also plead the mitigation of too many games? Be that as it may, the eagerly anticipated Wembley Final was never more than a hillock for Chelsea to surmount once Di Matteo had stormed his way into the record books with his spectacular 25-yard shot to find the roof of the 'Boro net after a mere 43 seconds. And although Chelsea kept their admirers waiting for a further 80 minutes before Zola's magic gave Newton a chance to settle matters by steering the ball into the net with his left foot, Middlesbrough were seldom a serious threat. The long 25-year drought was over!

Sadly, Zola did not illuminate the occasion as had been hoped. Hughes, claiming his fourth FA Cup winners' medal, was less dominant than in earlier rounds and Chelsea's overall superiority was not reflected by the margin of victory. Probably too much had been expected? Not that the massive Blue Army were concerned with such trivia. Victory was sweet for

Gianfranco Zola hits a free-kick over the Middlesbrough wall at Wembley. Zola's free-kicks from anywhere within 35 yards of an opponent's goal always bring a sense of anticipation from Chelsea's fans.

It's ours! Skipper Dennis Wise shows the FA Cup to Chelsea's adoring fans.

those who had patiently waited so long, and next day the open-topped bus was once more wending its way through those packed SW streets, a journey some doubted they would ever see again.

Europe was again beckoning and Ruud Gullit's first venture into management had ended in triumph. Never one to blow his own trumpet, he modestly summed it up. "A very professional performance. Mr Bates deserves it …also for Matthew Harding. We feel he is still with us. For me it has been a dream."

Apart from Graham Le Saux returning 'home' after more than four years at Blackburn, where he had won 20 international caps, the autumn of 1997 saw a cluster of new faces entering the Chelsea changing room from the other side of the Channel, and beyond.

Dutchman Ed de Goey became the third international goalkeeper on the books; Gustave Poyet had already shown his mettle when he played against Chelsea for Real Zaragoza in the European Cup-winners' Cup semi-final of 1995; the Nigerian teenager Celestine Babayaro cost £2.25 million, having made a big impression as a left-side player at Anderlecht; while Tore Andre Flo, 15 caps for Norway, arrived to challenge for a striking place alongside Zola, Mark Hughes and Vialli. Two others, lesser names perhaps, Bernard Lambourde and Laurent Charvet, completed a powerful squad in which no one could claim his first-team place by right.

Or as Ruud Gullit put it: "Selection is becoming bigger and bigger and bigger and we love it."

Even so, there was never any suggestion that all would be plain sailing. Manchester United won the FA Charity Shield after a penalty 'shoot-out'. And any further trace of complacency was banished when the opening Premiership fixture, at Coventry, was carelessly tossed away.

Despite the primary target remaining the Premiership 'Crown', never once did Chelsea manage to lead the pack throughout the nine-month season. Still the ingrained habit of performing below par against opposition of lesser pretensions remained the trait which has infuriated and frustrated supporters down the years.

Chelsea manager Ruud Gullit holds aloft the FA Cup to underline the fact that he is the most successful 'foreign' manager in the history of English football.

Ruud Gullit — Peerless Maestro

NOT since Tommy Lawton strode into Stamford Bridge 50 years earlier had any new arrival created anything like the excitement generated by the signing of Ruud Gullit.

The first appearance of the then reigning England centre-forward, still serving in the Army and with his Brylcreemed hair, promptly added some 22,000 on to the attendance figure. Ruud, far more relaxed and laid back, made a similarly instant impact, settling into his unfamiliar surroundings immediately, aided by his friendship with Glenn Hoddle with whom he shared his new manager's attitude and beliefs on how the game should be played.

Originally, the plan was for the 33-year old Dutchman to operate as a sweeper, a role for which he was eminently suited, and which it was hoped would prolong his playing career.

Circumstances, however, dictated otherwise. Young Michael Duberry forced his way on to the scene as a defender of unusual promise, and David Lee re-established his place in the side when he deputised, following injury to Gullit which kept the great man out of action for half a dozen games, indirectly causing his move into the central midfield area for the first time in his life, and from where he could exert an even stronger influence.

He excited crowds wherever he played. His mastery of the ball was total, whether bringing it under instant control, or effortlessly passing it with deadly accuracy to a colleague 50 or 60 yards distant.

Ever the professor, the perfectionist, his extraordinary talents constantly brought gasps of astonishment from crowds up and down the country. His manager was delighted. "A magnificent capture on and off the pitch. A terrific professional through and through. It is lovely to see the way he has moulded in."

And it caused little surprise, following Hoddle's somewhat sudden departure to take control of the England team, that Chelsea immediately turned to Gullit to step into Glenn's shoes, after only one season's experience of English football, to fulfill a double role as player-manager.

Ever the realist, he was well conscious of the burden he was inheriting. "I know it won't be easy," he announced. "But Glenn has provided a good basis and that should make it a little easier." There were no rash promises.

Soon, fate had dealt the great man a harsh deal (or was it a helping hand in disguise?). Injuries kept Ruud off the pitch for the majority of the 1996-97 season, allowing him to concentrate on orchestrating his ever-increasing talented squad of players from a distance.

On taking office he had announced, "I am simply hoping for a good year starting with our next game. At the end of the season it would be nice to be thinking about trophies."

He was certainly as good as his word as the FA Cup found its way into the Chelsea trophy cabinet nine months later. Now, under his unique style of managership, a period of stability in this office, after the many comings and goings at Chelsea, seemed assured.

But, then the bombshell. Always his own man, and apparently unwilling to meet the club's hierarchy to discuss his own future and personal demands, he was unceremoniously dismissed amid a flurry of accusations from both sides.

None the less, he will remain a formidable name in the Chelsea story. The club's greatest player? And most successful manager?

Graham Le Saux and Manchester United's David Beckham in action.

Eddie Newton tries to stop Aston Villa's Savo Milosevic.

Lancashire, especially, proved infertile territory. Visits to Manchester United, Liverpool, Bolton, Blackburn and Everton produced merely a single point. Such troughs of form contrasted vividly with other memorable displays of highly inventive skills.

The defences of Barnsley and Tottenham were each penetrated six times in front of their own supporters. Few will forget the total domination of Derby County, comprehensively outplayed at The Bridge at the end of November when away supporters gave Zola a standing ovation as he left the field following his hat-trick. Or of Arsenal's elimination from the League Cup two months later, Chelsea

overturning a one-goal deficit from the first 'leg' at Highbury. In April, Liverpool, too, were sent home empty-handed after a second half display of awesome power by this exciting Chelsea team.

But, as ever, the necessary consistency in the bread-and-butter Premiership competition was found wanting and it was to 'knock-out' football where Chelsea turned for rewards.

The (Coca-Cola) League Cup campaign opened in a low key. Having been excused entry until the third round, the Chelsea team confronting Blackburn contained only three players who had appeared in the previous Premiership fixture. Having surmounted this hurdle, (via a penalty 'shoot-out'), and the following tie with Southampton (after extra-time), again with an unfamiliar line-up, and in the shadow of early elimination from the FA Cup, policy changed for the quarter-final confrontation with Ipswich Town in Suffolk. Four days earlier, Manchester United had humiliated Chelsea, coasting to a five-goal lead at Stamford Bridge before a somewhat meaningless late three-goal revival at least salvaged some measure of self-respect.

But it was another 'shoot-out' at Portman Road which was required to set up the two-leg semi-final meeting with Arsenal. At Highbury, Chelsea were rescued from near-oblivion thanks to a typical Mark Hughes headed goal which enabled the 2-1 deficit to be wiped out in an outstanding display in the second chapter – Chelsea emerging winners, 4-3 on aggregate, having played probably their best football of the season.

A third Wembley appearance in little over ten months saw a repeat of the 1997 FA Cup Final. Middlesbrough the opposition; 2-0 the score, with extra-time goals from Frank Sinclair's header and Roberto Di Matteo (again).

Frank Sinclair scores for Chelsea against Middlesbrough in the 1998 Coca-Cola Cup Final at Wembley.

A besuited Gianluca Vialli with the Coca-Cola Cup.

By then, however, Chelsea had attracted attention from matters off the field. On Thursday, 12 February, Ruud Gullit was dismissed as manager of Chelsea Football Club following a disagreement over renewal of contract.

The Dutch international had demanded a two-year player-coach agreement; the club were pressing for a three-year coaching-only settlement which had been 'on the table' for some five months. Further, Gullit was demanding a greatly increased financial deal. And an additional complication appeared to be the difficulty of actually enticing him to a meeting to discuss terms. Sadly, from every point of view, Ruud's 32 months at Stamford Bridge therefore ended in acrimony amid accusation and counter accusation.

Capped by Holland on 65 occasions, and respected and admired throughout the world of football for his outstanding flair and ability, he was probably the most gifted, and versatile, player ever to represent Chelsea, even if his magical performances were virtually confined to his first season.

His management style was unusual, if not unique, and certainly strange to British ways. But the 1997 FA Cup Final victory and his steering of the club towards two further major trophies in 1998 is a compelling justification of such methods.

Within 24 hours Gianluca Vialli had been appointed as Gullit's replacement, to the surprise of almost everyone. Another whose skill and achievements were acknowledged universally, his first season at Chelsea had not been without its problems.

Lack of fitness, and injuries, confined him to the substitutes' bench for much of the 1996-97 campaign, despite being Chelsea's leading goalscorer in the Premiership. Already a cult figure with the fans, he was certainly not always in harmony with his manager.

At the time of writing, the jury's verdict on Vialli's appointment remains open, but no one could have made a bigger or more immediate impact in his new

Frank Lebeouf battles in the snow with a Tromso forward as Chelsea show great character in terrible conditions.

Tore Andre Flo and Marquez of Real Betis in the European Cup-winners' Cup tie.

role. First, that semi-final victory against Arsenal. Then the League Cup, won at Wembley with the new manager relegating himself to watch from the side-lines. And, finally, the gala evening in Stockholm.

Throughout the season Chelsea had been many people's favourites to repeat their European triumph of 1971 and, if their progress towards that goal was not without incident and moments of doubt, they mostly had matters under control.

From the start with Slovan Bratislava, they profited by the knowledge and experience of European football acquired by their foreign contingent.

The blinding blizzard in the Arctic wastes in Tromso provided one unexpected examination, and only Tore Flo's important early goals against Real Betis enabled the next hurdle to be cleared less easily than the scoreline suggests.

It was Vicenza, however, who produced the stiffest examination. Their 1-0 lead in Italy did not appear a decisive advantage – at least not until they doubled this margin after half an hour's play at The Bridge. Indeed, it took a brilliant 20-yard volley from Poyet soon afterwards to keep hope alive; a hope justified when Zola, dashing through the middle of the park, launched himself into a header to convert Vialli's cross, after his own high-speed incursion down the right flank.

Heady stuff; but even more was to follow. With Chelsea at last in control, Mark Hughes fastened on to de Goey's long kick out and deftly headed the ball over a central defender before lashing a magnificent left-foot volley past a helpless goalkeeper and into the far corner of the net. An unforgettable, and ultimately deserved, passport into the Final.

Three weeks can seem an eternity in football. Premiership matches to be faced, obligations to be met and, most worrying of all, injuries to be attended to. As it was, Wise, Zola and Le Saux spent most of that interval on the treatment table (Zola in Italy) and Le Saux in fact lost the battle against the clock.

Stockholm's Rasunda Stadium entered the annals of Chelsea Football Club's history on a gloriously sunny evening of early summer. The magnificent city had been swamped by the Blue Army soon after dawn. Sixteen thousand strong? Twenty thousand? Or more? All were in party mood. Almost more importantly of all, everyone behaved impeccably.

The arrival of the grim-faced riot police squads outside the stadium, some three hours before kick-off, seemed, and was, totally out of context with the occasion.

Within minutes, however, the atmosphere changed from one of tense uncertainty and suspicion to a mood of partying and celebration. Cameras were produced and clicked as Chelsea fans of both sexes lined up for endless photographs with the police, who gradually realised that their presence was required for social purposes only rather than anything more serious – their hostile expressions soon melting into smiles and relaxation.

The game itself, as so often on these occasions, never lived up to its billing, for the most part its quality disappointing. Tension and drama? Yes. But, at least the only goal of the contest will ever be recalled by the 30,000 present, and many thousands more riveted to their television screens.

Chelsea, having recovered from a nervous, error-strewn beginning, only gradually assumed a measure of control. And it took the intervention of Graham Rix, Vialli's touch-line 'director', to settle matters with an inspired substitution.

Zola, following his weeks of treatment, and omitted from the starting line-up, was summoned to replace Flo (Vialli apparently not taking kindly to the suggestion that he, himself, should retire from the

Stuttgart's Thomas Schneider is beaten by Flo in the Cup-winners' Cup Final in Stockholm.

Gianfranco Zola whose stunning goal gave Chelsea the Cup-winners' Cup for the second time in the club's history.

trophies, those nightmare years of the late 1970s a distant memory. Relegation had followed four years after Athens as CFC fell apart and almost disappeared altogether.

Now, of course, everything has been revolutionised. A new ambitious chairman who has not only built a 21st-century stadium but a 'village complex' too; income flows in from a multitude of different quarters. The future would appear rosier (or should it be bluer?) than ever before.

Nevertheless, new challenges lie ahead. Three trophies have just been acquired, yes. But the 1997-98 season also produced no fewer than 15 Premiership defeats. A defence which, not least in Stockholm, has repeatedly proved shaky and prone to error, needs bolstering.

The team is not a youthful one. Mark Hughes, Steve Clarke, Petrescu, Poyet, Wise and, of course, Vialli himself, are all past 30. And Hughes is reportedly on his way from The Bridge as this is written.

Gianluca, as manager, will be only too well aware that his next target must be an assault on the Premiership title itself. And to this end new signings to augment Chelsea's already bulging overseas contingent (13 at the end of the 1997-98 season) are already in place.

Encouragingly, too, promising young talent exists in the junior ranks. New names are filtering into the first team – Morris, Hanley, Crittenden. A trickle as yet, but one that, hopefully, will increase.

The days of Jimmy Thompson's scouring for skills on Hackney Marshes will never return, but the similar injections of youthful promise to accompany high-cost cheque-book signings from further afield would be warmly welcomed.

Meanwhile, all is hope and optimism.

scene). Acquainting himself with the ball immediately, Zola next fastened on to Wise's incisive through pass to strike a powerful, and totally unstoppable, winning goal. This, only 24 seconds (or was it 22?) after entering the fray.

And so Stockholm 1998 is bracketed with Athens 1971. Now, 12 months had provided three major

Dennis Wise and his Chelsea team mates celebrate victory in Stockholm.